The Story of Peter, Ruth and Evan
Knowing Good and Evil

By:

Fauneil Fremont

ISBN: 978-1-965951-19-4 (sc)

Seraphim Global Media LLC 155 Willow brook Blvd Ste 110
Wayne, NJ 07470
848 800 6538
fullfillment@seraphimgml.com

"Reason and Faith

should be complementary fields

for man

in search of truth."

C. S. Lewis

TABLE OF CONTENTS:

Preface by Author

The Writing of *Peter, Ruth, and Evan*

To the reader:

In a sense, I have been writing this book since childhood. I was raised in a Christian home in rural Nebraska, where my parents and grandparents based their lives, to the best of their ability, on "The Ten Commandments." Until high school, I attended parochial school, where the emphasis was on "The New Testament" and Christ's two commandments: (1) Love God with all your heart, soul, and mind; and (2) Love your neighbor as yourself.

During high school, college, and early adulthood, literature and music became my primary interests. Piano performance and a career as an English teacher followed. Along the way, I was fortunate to meet a young man who had a Christian background and who was also interested in music and literature, both sacred and secular. We married, had one child, and lived in California for most of our years together.

At age forty-one, while teaching English, I was *called* to become a church organist. I studied for ten years with Richard Purvis, a renowned composer and organist at Grace Cathedral in San Francisco; at the same time, I returned to college to attain a B.A. and an M.A. in organ performance. During my thirty-six years as an organist/choir director, I worked with hundreds of people experiencing the joys of baptism and marriage or their sorrows of death and bereavement. Throughout the years, I have been employed in Lutheran, Episcopal, Anglican and Methodist churches; I have dealt with a dozen ministers (pastors or rectors) and many counselors and staff members. Thus, I have had experience in looking at scripture and religion from different points of view.

In my novel, I have patterned Peter and Reverend Howard after ministers and counselors I have admired. Ruth is patterned after me, only in relation to her interests and skills. All of the characters are fictional, as well as the Martin home in Los Gatos, the Edward Mills Christian Retirement Residence (the "center" in the delta), God's Bounty Mission in Oakland, Grace Christian Church in Lodi, E & J Pet Shelter in Sacramento, E & W Land Developers in the Sierra Nevada Mountains, and St. Paul's Seminary at Berkeley.

I hope that you enjoy this figment of my imagination, based on some autobiographical experiences.

Happy reading! Fauneil

* * *

Chapter I: Re-engagement

It was a lovely evening in Los Gatos, California. Ruth Martin had parked her blue hatch-back Mini Cooper in the Los Gatos High School parking lot. She walked along the front of the building, which sat back from the street, surrounded by a lush emerald-green lawn. Remembering her four student years here, eating lunch with her friend Betsy, she felt thankful for that joyful time. She was on her way to meet Betsy, whom she hadn't seen in seven years. Betsy had married and was living in Santa Fe, New Mexico; Ruth had graduated from the University of California in Berkeley with a degree in psychology and had returned to Los Gatos to live with her parents while she fulfilled her counseling requirements to become a therapist.

When school was out for the day, Ruth and Betsy had often walked this route to get a snack from the corner boulangerie located opposite a small park, where they sat on a bench near a fountain shaded by redwoods. From this spot, they could share their experiences of the day and chat about fellow classmates as they passed by.

Ruth had agreed to meet Betsy by the old bank, with its hanging outdoor clock, located across from the boulangerie. When Ruth had walked past a row of quaint shops and across a bridge over Highway 17, she heard brass and woodwind instruments warming up for the concert in the park. At the end of another block, she saw Betsy waiting under the clock.

"Betsy," exclaimed Ruth. "You look just the same — no, lovelier. Marriage agrees with you."

"And you look like you're ready for the professional world. Are you through with school now?"

"Yes, with classrooms. I'm studying people now. Say, let's see if we can find a seat on one of our old benches for the concert. Look, over there by the fountain."

As they waited for the concert to begin, their conversation first centered on Betsy: her marriage to Bill, whom Ruth remembered from Los Gatos High, and their two children. Betsy had come prepared with photos of a four-year-old boy, smiling, with a few front teeth missing, and a chubby, rosy-cheeked two-year-old girl.

Ruth then filled Betsy in briefly with her last seven years. Her college days had been a combination of hard work, activities, and casual dating (no true love yet). She had spent summer vacations with her parents, who had taken her on trips to Victoria, Banff, and Lake Louise in Canada.

"How are your parents?" asked Betsy.

"Fine. Dad is as busy as usual. He has to travel a lot, but now Mom can go with him. She doesn't have to be 'the hen watching over her chick.'" Betsy smiled.

"Ruth, look at that young man on the other side of the fountain, the one with the blond hair. Isn't that Evan Lancaster from Los Gatos High?"

"Yes. He was one of those stuck on himself seniors when we were freshmen. I dated him once at Berkeley. He didn't call me again. Good riddance! He was still self-centered."

When the band concert ended, Ruth and Betsy strolled past the old opera house, which had been converted into an antique shop. At the corner, they crossed the street and walked past St. Luke's Episcopal Church to Old Town, which had been converted from an elementary school complex into chic shops and restaurants. They headed for the Wine Cellar. Going down several steps, they entered an underground restaurant/bar. The space was intimate, with only two small rooms, one with the bar and small tables, and a second with more small tables and a raised area with long tables and bench seating. The low lights, wood, brick walls and tile floors created the ambience of a grotto. Ruth ordered a plate of hors d'oeuvres and a carafe of Sauvignon Blanc.

As they sat sipping their wine, Betsy said, "There he is again."

"Who? Where?"

"Evan Lancaster. Two tables behind you. He's with a guy I don't recognize."

"I'm not going to look. I hope he doesn't see us."

But Evan did see them. As he and the "guy" were leaving, they stopped at their table. "Ruth Martin!" exclaimed Evan. "Do you still live in Los Gatos?"

"Yes. You remember Betsy?"

Evan nodded and said, "This is my friend Emile Romero from Oakland."   Romero waved 'hello' and said, "I have a plane to catch. 'Bye, ladies. So long, Evan." Evan patted him on the shoulder and turned back to re-engage Ruth.

"So, you came back to Los Gatos after Berkeley?"

"Yes. I'm living with my parents until I complete the requirements to become a therapist."

"Do your parents still live on Kennedy Road?"

"Yes, up in the hills."

"I'm in the San Joaquin Valley now, but I come often to the San Jose area on business. Maybe we'll meet again." He smiled broadly, shook hands with each of them, and left.

"Wow!" exclaimed Betsy. "What a hunk! Those broad shoulders. His blond hair, blue eyes, tanned skin. He didn't seem to be stuck on himself, Ruth."

"I agree," she said. "Perhaps the business world has taken some of the arrogance out of him."

Chapter II: At Vasona Lake

Ruth drove into the public lot at Vasona Lake and parked near the playground and depot, where the open-air scenic train was puffing away. She attached a leash to the collar of her chestnut brown dachshund, took out a picnic basket from the hatchback, and headed for the grassy area around the lake. On the way to the lake, the scenic railroad, with its passengers of adults and excited children, chugged by. As Ruth's dog barked, one of the children waved and yelled, "What's his name?" "Posie," Ruth shouted back.

"Let's stroll around the lake, Posie, before we eat our lunch." Posie shook herself and wagged her tail. As they approached the lake, Posie became excited and barked at the white ducks swimming near the water's edge. Farther out, Ruth could see a paddle boat with a man and two boys. Because the boys were struggling over the control of the steering wheel, the boat was going around in a hopeless circle. Ruth watched as the adult finally took hold of the wheel and headed the boat towards shore.

Ruth turned around and walked through the grass until the lake disappeared. Then she spread out the tablecloth from her basket and took out the food, bottled water, and Posie's bowl. She opened one of the bottles and poured some into the bowl and drank the rest herself. She freed Posie from the leash, seated herself on the cloth, and opened a wrapped sandwich of bologna and cheese.

Ruth and Posie were sharing the sandwich when they saw a group of picnickers approaching: two men and two boys. She recognized one of the men and the boys as the paddle boaters on the lake. As the second man came closer, she realized that it was Evan Lancaster.

"Ruth!" he exclaimed. "Here you are again!"

"Yes, it's not just the Wine Cellar I frequent."

"Lucky for me. Ruth, this is my friend, Marv Springer, and his two sons. Marv, Ruth Martin." Ruth nodded at Marv and glanced at the boys. "I enjoyed watching you paddleboat on the lake," she said. Marv shrugged and responded, "One of the joys of being a father of a five-year-old and a four-year-old." He pointed to his sons. "Meet Seth and Sam."

"Can we play with your dog?" Seth asked.

"Yes. Her name is Posie. She's a dachshund, and she loves to play ball." Ruth reached into her basket and handed Seth a soft leather ball.

"Stay where we can see you," ordered Marv as the two ran off.

"Do you want to sit down a while to watch them play? I brought along a thermos of coffee and some paper cups."

"Thank you," Evan answered for them. "Seth and Sam are two cute kids. Marv is doing a good job raising them."

"Only part-time. I have them every other weekend," Marv explained to Ruth. She surmised that Marv was either divorced or a widower, and she politely did not pursue Marv's personal life. Evan changed the subject. "How long have you had Posie, Ruth?"

"For three years. Our last family dog died of old age, and we immediately replaced her with Posie. She's the third dachsie we've had."

"What does your family like about that breed?" inquired Marv. "I'm thinking of getting a dog for my boys."

"My mother likes the fact that she is shorthaired and doesn't shed. Also, Mom likes a lapdog, one she can cuddle. So do I, and Dad likes her because she is smart and doesn't yap much."

"Most men prefer big dogs, don't they?" asked Marv.

"I guess so. However, my dad isn't interested in sports and doesn't want a dog for hunting or protection. Besides, my parents like to travel, and a dachsie doesn't dominate a car, like a big dog does. So, the car doesn't always smell like 'dog.'"

"Consequently, you have a pleasant-smelling, perfect, portable Posie!" remarked Evan.

"Yes. A playful, pleasant-smelling, perfect, portable Posie," responded Ruth. Playful Posie came running back to lap up water from her bowl, followed by her playmates. Marv arose, looked at his watch, and announced that he had promised to get the boys home by five o'clock.

"Ruth, I enjoyed the coffee and the conversation. Evan, see you soon." After they had left, Ruth asked Evan if he was hungry and brought out two more wrapped sandwiches from her basket, one for Evan and another to share with Posie.

"I'm really happy to have seen you by chance," said Evan. "I wanted to contact you, but I had neither a telephone number nor an email address for you, and I didn't know where you live on Kennedy Road." He paused. "Ruth, how about another picnic next Saturday?"

"At Vasona?"

"I was thinking of a drive to Carmel and then continuing south on Highway 1 until we find a spot to picnic."

"That sounds beautiful. I love that area."

"Good. We can take my car. I'll bring the food and wine for a picnic on a bluff overlooking the ocean." Evan walked Posie and Ruth to her car. He exchanged phone numbers with her and jotted down her address in his contact book. "I'll call you Friday evening to discuss the details," he said as he gave Posie a goodbye pat and Ruth a high-five.

When Ruth and Posie returned home, her mother asked her if she had enjoyed Vasona.

"Yes. I saw a classmate from Los Gatos High. Evan Lancaster."

"I don't remember your talking about him."

"I found him very conceited then, but he's changed for the better."

"How so?"

"He's friendly and outgoing now; he enjoys kids, dogs, and picnics."

"My goodness, Ruth! Can he be real?"

Chapter III: Carmel

Ruth and her mother watched from a picture window as Evan drove his Austin Healey through the wrought iron gates and up the driveway, to park under the portico.

"I hope he can afford that sports car," Mrs. Martin observed.

"I'll know soon enough," responded Ruth as she went to answer the doorbell. Ruth led him through the entrance, past the curved stairs, to the lounge where Mrs. Martin had seated herself with Posie in her lap. Ruth introduced her mother and invited Evan to sit down. Posie remembered him and came to sit by his feet. Evan reached down and took her onto his lap. As Evan and Mrs. Martin engaged in chit-chat, he looked around the room: an expensive Kashan rug on the parquet floor, a large stone fireplace with three comfortable traditional sofas arranged in a U-shape in front of the fire, a rosewood grand piano in one corner, and oil paintings decorating the room.

"This is a lovely, warm room," remarked Evan. "How long have you lived here, Mrs. Martin?"

"Since shortly after my husband joined a corporate law firm in San Jose. Ruth was about three at the time."

"Oh, is that a portrait of Ruth holding a dachshund?" he asked, pointing to the mantle.

"Yes, that's Ruth and Heinie, our first dachsie. Heinie was a darling. She had been sired by a champion."

"After Heinie died, I convinced my parents to get a shelter dog," explained Ruth.

"Ruthie has always been gentle-hearted," said Mrs. Martin.

"We'd better leave," said Ruth, "before Mom starts bragging about me." Mrs. Martin smiled, arose, and took Posie from Evan as she escorted them to the door.

Kennedy Road was not far from Highway 17, which led across the Santa Cruz Mountains to Santa Cruz and Highway 1, the coastal highway. Because Highway 17 ascended and then descended rapidly, the vehicles faced steep ravines and granite cliffs on opposite sides. There was nowhere to go in case of an emergency. Ruth had always been frightened whenever she had traveled to Santa Cruz. Now, riding in the low Austin Healey, among sedans, SUVs, and trucks, she became increasingly anxious. Evan was taking risks by weaving in and out of the traffic. He was undoubtedly an expert at changing gears and handling the clutch, accelerator and brake, but Ruth was not impressed. *Is he showing off*, she wondered, but she said nothing.

When they reached Highway 1, the road became level, and Evan drove fast but sensibly. On the way to Carmel, they drove through the seaside towns of Aptos, Capitola, and Moss Landing. At Castroville, they were in agricultural country where artichokes were growing in the fields. As they neared Carmel, Evan asked Ruth if she wanted to take the 17-Mile-Drive to Pebble Beach.

"No, I've seen the golf course, and I prefer the sites along Highway 1," she answered.

"How about a quick drive through Carmel and past the Carmel Mission and then back to the highway?"

"O.K. I always enjoy driving by there. Did you see the painting of the mission in our lounge? It's one of my favorites." Evan answered *no*. Back on the highway, they soon came to the two-lane area which would lead to Big Sur. The road wound through granite cliffs on the left and steep ravines on the right, leading down to a rocky shoreline with smashing waves. Evan began weaving again, and Ruth became anxious again.

"How can we possibly picnic here?" she asked.

"Just wait and see; it's just past the Bixby Bridge." Evan turned into a driveway where a restaurant was set back from the highway, but within sight and sound of the ocean. He parked and escorted Ruth to the outdoor deck of the restaurant.

"Surprise! Picnic time!"

"Picnic here, at a restaurant?"

"Yes, overlooking the ocean, listening to the crashing of the waves, and eating a chef-prepared picnic: your choice of sand dabs, crab cakes, or sole, Madam!" Ruth smiled.

"I hope they serve sourdough bread while we're waiting, Evan."

During their lunch, Ruth asked Evan to fill in the gaps of time since high school.

"You know that I graduated from Los Gatos High when you were a freshman there. I graduated with honors and was accepted at Berkeley. We dated once during your freshman year there, remember?" She nodded. "I should have been in my senior year, but I had played around too much. It took me two more years to graduate. Finally, my father put his foot down and issued an ultimatum: Buckle down or get out!"

"So, your father was a disciplinarian?" Ruth asked.

"No. He just didn't want to keep paying the bills. He was the captain of a cruise ship based in San Diego. I only saw him during summer vacations when he allowed me for a brief time on board, which was hardly a disciplined environment."

"What was that like, living on a cruise ship?"

"A lot of loafing around: swimming, video games, shuffle board, bingo, night club acts, gambling, meeting wealthy people and some very 'seedy' characters. No wonder I needed to buckle down."

"Where did you live during the school year?"

"While at Berkeley, in the dorm. In Los Gatos, with my grandparents. When my mother died, my father left the military service to become the captain of the cruise ship."

"Are your grandparents still living?"

"My grandfather passed on at age sixty. My grandmother lived alone for a number of years until she moved into the retirement center in the San Joaquin Valley, where I'm the financial director."

"What was it like, growing up in your grandparents' home?"

"That requires a lengthy explanation. To give you just a glimpse of it, my grandmother wanted me to call her 'Gloria'. The name 'grandmother' made her too old, and she knew that she could never take the place of 'Mom.' So, 'Gloria' it was."

"Your background is quite different from mine. I had a stable home, steady parental supervision, a lack of adversities, and a pampered childhood."

"Background isn't everything, Ruth. I'm putting the past behind me."

Ruth lifted her wineglass and said, "Good for you, Evan. Best foot forward!"

Chapter IV: Evan's Mission

As Ruth waited for Evan in the lounge of her home, her parents entered the room.

"Where are you going today?" Mrs. Martin asked.

"First to Oakland to visit a neighborhood mission called 'God's Bounty.' Evan is the financial director of the mission."

"Rather a spiritual endeavor for a young sports car enthusiast," commented her mother.

"I doubt that being a financial director of a mission would be a very lucrative job," added her father.

"It's not. His main job is Director of Finance at the Forward in Faith Foundation and Treasurer at the Edward Mills Christian Retirement Residence, located in the San Joaquin Valley."

"That's a mouthful," quipped her mother.

When Evan arrived, Ruth introduced him to her father and engaged in small talk for a few minutes before explaining that they had a long day ahead of them. Following Oakland, they were going to San Francisco. She would be home late. "Don't wait up for me," she said upon leaving.

Evan and Ruth headed north on Highway 85 until Cupertino, where they took Highway 101 across the Dumbarton Bridge to Highway 880 and into Oakland. As they exited the freeway, Ruth asked Evan how he had gotten interested in charity work.

"I have a friend who grew up in the projects in West Oakland. Emile Romero – you met him at the Wine cellar. Do you know the Acorn Re-development Projects?"

"No. Were they housing for the poor?"

"Yes. The projects are in a slum area of Oakland. In 1962, the city's plan was to buy up old, dilapidated houses, many owned by blacks, tear them down, and build three modern housing units. The people evicted from their homes had to relocate to other areas of the city. Many of them fought eviction, but lost in a court battle. Unfortunately, once the houses had been demolished, the new units were not immediately erected; so, rats and other vermin moved into the area. About ten years later, the projects were finally completed. Most of the units were built for families needing two or more bedrooms; no low-cost apartments were available in the area for single working people. The only low-cost housing for singles was the Claridge Hotel, which had its origins during the Great Depression. It had been built as an Evangeline Home."

"What is an Evangeline Home?" asked Ruth.

"During the depression, the Salvation Army built group homes to help young working women. They provided a private room, a communal living room and dining room, and spiritual guidance. By 1956, young women wanted their independence, and the Evangeline Home became a hotel. However, the need for economic and spiritual guidance still exists. So, Emile and I started a mission to offer the neighborhood food, clothing, and a sanctuary."

"A noble endeavor," Ruth commented.

Evan had been driving on Brush Avenue and now turned off onto 15th Street. They passed the Claridge, whose chiseled stonework around the entrance door and Romanesque first-story windows hinted at a better past. Evan said, "It's just a few blocks from here to God's Bounty Mission."

Evan parked in front of the mission, a small building that had once been a 'mom-and-pop' convenience store. When they entered, Emile greeted them and introduced Ruth to his wife, Isabel. Emile showed them around the single room: racks of used clothing and reading materials at one end of the room; a kitchenette at the other; near the door, a table with donuts, bananas, apples, coffee, juice, and water; in the center of the room, a small table holding a crucifix, a Bible, a prayer book, and a basket for collections. Folding chairs were set in a circle around the table.

"What's your program like?" asked Ruth. Emile answered.

"We're open every day from 9:00 a.m. to 11:00 a.m. and from 1:00 a.m. to 3:00 p.m. During the first hour of each session, people can have refreshments and look through the reading materials or the clothing racks or visit with each other. During the second hour, we start with a scripture lesson, then a short homily followed by questions, answers, or sharing. We close with prayer."

"Do you both share the duties here?" Ruth asked Emile and Isabel.

"I look after the food and clothing. Emile is the primary spiritual leader, but we both pray and offer guidance. When Emile is gone, I take his place completely," responded Isabel.

"How's the attendance?" asked Evan.

"We have a lot of walk-ins, but some regulars, too," answered Emile.

"Keep up the good work," encouraged Evan. He glanced at his watch. "I'm sorry we can't stay. We're headed for San Francisco."

"I'm glad you both stopped in today. Come again."

As they were leaving Oakland, Ruth said to Evan, "That was interesting. I hope your mission is successful. Emile and Isabel seem nice. How did you and Emile happen to meet?"

"As I told you, when I was in high school, my father became the captain of a cruise ship. Emile was working as a cabin boy on the ship. We became friends and larked about when Emile was off duty. Since my father didn't want me bothering him, he allowed me to go anywhere on the ship, either alone or with a companion. Sometimes Emile and I played ship games. At other times, we were allowed into the casino or the night club. Whenever the ship docked at a port, we joined a group of sightseers for a shore excursion. We definitely enjoyed the lifestyle of the rich!"

"I thought that I was the spoiled child, but you were allowed a lot of freedom for a teenager. So, how did you come out of that to take an interest in the poor?"

"During the school year, I kept in touch with Emile. Following my graduation from Los Gatos High, Emile got us jobs in a soup kitchen run by the Salvation Army."

"What was that like? Did you get to know any of the people who came to eat?"

"Occasionally, but most of them were just hungry and solemn. They were down on their luck and living one step away from a tent city."

"What's a tent city?" asked Ruth.

"It's an area where the homeless group together, living in tents and tarps, without running water. Trash and feces can be lying about, and an overwhelming smell of urine is in the air."

"Oh, I've seen that when San Francisco or Oakland is in the news. My parents and I have discussed it. I feel sorry for the homeless; but I also understand why businesses, homeowners, landlords, and renters pressure the authorities to evict the campers. The area belongs to them, too. My dad says it is a crisis without a simple resolution. There is so much economic inequality. The breach between the rich and the poor continues to widen."

"Yes," agreed Evan. "City officials only have short-term solutions. They can do things, like moving in jagged rocks, making it difficult to set up tents or to move around. Once in a while, they do a 'deep cleaning'."

"What's that?" Ruth asked.

"They come in and remove all the trash, destroy the rats and vermin, thoroughly wash and spray the area, and evict the homeless. But that is only temporary. Eviction doesn't work."

"How so?"

"During the day, the homeless leave with their clothing, tarp, or sometimes a mattress on the top of a shopping cart. They can't go far; so, they come back at night. If they are moved out of the city, other destitute people soon replace them."

"Economic inequality isn't the only issue. Drugs, illegal immigrants, mental illness, unemployment are all part of the crisis. My dad says that it will take another crisis to solve this crisis," said Ruth.

"In the meantime, Emile and I are trying to help the vulnerable with our mission, at least some people who are not yet lost."

Chapter V: San Francisco

While crossing the Bay Bridge, Evan relayed his next plan. "We're going to the Top of the Mark for dinner, but instead of driving up Nob Hill, I'm going to park the car near the beginning of the trolley line, and we'll take the trolley up. I don't want to burn out the clutch or the brakes in my car."

As they exited the trolley car at the top of the hill, the Fairmont Hotel was on their right, the Mark Hopkins on their left, and Grace Cathedral was a block away.

"Our dinner reservation is in an hour," informed Evan, looking at his watch.

"We have time to walk through the park to Grace Cathedral," suggested Ruth.

"O.K. I've driven past but never entered," Evan admitted.

"I've been to the cathedral numerous times with my parents for worship services, organ concerts, and social occasions. I'll give you a quick tour." As they approached, Ruth drew his attention to the huge 16-foot-high, gilded bronze entrance doors. "They are called the 'Doors of Paradise' and are world-famous replicas of the doors created for the Baptistery of the Florence Cathedral in Itay in the 15th century." Entering the vestibule and standing at the beginning of the nave, she pointed out that there were three aisles, a wide central one and two narrower side aisles. Before continuing, Ruth explained that Grace Cathedral is a Gothic style cathedral, an architectural style dating back to the Medieval Period.

"Can you explain *Gothic?*" Evan asked.

"Basically, Gothic cathedrals were built in the shape of the cross. You can see only part of the shape as you walk around the cathedral, but if you visualize the cathedral from above, you see that the central aisle of the long nave is the vertical beam of the cross, and the transept is the horizontal beam. The sanctuary is in the middle of the transept. It is the most sacred part of the cathedral because it contains the high altar. The sanctuary is patterned after the central part of the cross, where the crucified body hung, with arms stretched out to left and right and nailed to the horizontal beam of the cross."

As they approached the sanctuary, Ruth pointed out the altar, which was surrounded by the communion railing and the kneeling area, with its beautiful needlepoint cushions. She drew Evan's attention to the seating in the side chapels, which faced the sanctuary so that everything was centered around the area, signifying the crucifixion. Ruth led Evan around the high altar, past the choir area, and towards the back of the cathedral, called the apse.

"The apse in a Gothic cathedral often has a semi-circular shape with a high dome above it. The ceiling may be decorated with a mural, and the curved walls usually contain beautiful stained-glass windows, like these. Did you notice the three rose windows near the top of the cathedral, Evan?" They looked up, and Ruth pointed them out. "From the outside of the cathedral, you can see that the apse is the end of the cathedral. Because of its height, flying buttresses are often built to hold up the structure. That is the case in the famous Notre Dame Cathedral in Paris."

"Good description," commented Evan. "You obviously understand a lot about cathedral architecture. Have you been to Notre Dame Cathedral?"

"Yes, with my parents, I toured the Gothic cathedrals in Chartres and Notre Dame in France. They both left me with the realization that Christians throughout centuries have been inspired by their faith to build and maintain these glorious places of worship."

"Grace Cathedral makes my little mission look like a joke," muttered Evan.

"Not at all," countered Ruth.

As they left, the cathedral bells escorted them all the way to the Mark Hopkins, where they took the elevator up to the top. In the revolving restaurant, Evan had reserved a table next to one of the picture windows surrounding the restaurant. It was early evening, and the city lights had not yet dominated the scene. Evan pointed out some of the landmarks: the Golden Gate Bridge, Sausalito, San Francisco Bay, Alcatraz, Fisherman's Wharf, and Quoit Tower. "From up here," he said, "you can't see any of the mess made by the street people."

"Yes," agreed Ruth. "We are among the privileged and fortunate."

***

The following day, Ruth visited with her mother about her experiences in Oakland and San Francisco. "It was a day of opposites for me," Ruth said, "the poverty in Oakland and the humble simplicity of Evan's mission contrasted by the elegance of Grace Cathedral and the sumptuous meal we had at the Top of the Mark."

"That kind of day makes you think about the inequality in the world," agreed Mrs. Martin. "How did Evan appear to relate to the contrast?"

"I'm not sure. He was hard to read. Perhaps I'll be able to learn more about him when he takes me on Saturday to the retirement home where he lives and works in the San Joaquin Valley."

***

On Saturday, Ruth dressed for the day's outing in slacks, a blouse, tennis shoes, a straw hat, and sunglasses. Evan motored east on Hwy 17 to Hwy 880 north, then Hwy 680 to Hwy 580 east to Hwy 5, followed by Hwy 12 to Rio Vista, and finally, Hwy 160 to the Sacramento-San Joaquin delta area.

"I'd never find the way by myself," said Ruth.

"We're almost there," responded Evan. As he left the paved highway and turned onto a gravel road, the habitat changed from agriculture to grasslands, woodland savannas, and wetlands.

"This is paradise for nature lovers," remarked Ruth. "Is there a wildlife refuge nearby?"

"Yes. The Stone Lakes Refuge is close. It is a haven for ducks, geese, sandhill cranes, sandpipers, and plovers. There is good fishing, too, for striped bass, sturgeon, catfish, bluegill, perch, and bullheads."

"Obviously, you enjoy fishing." Ruth said. Evan nodded.

"What are those plants alongside the road?" Ruth asked.

"They're called *cattails*. They're planted to keep the land from sinking. Some of the land here is twenty feet below the surrounding water. When the plants die, they build up peat, which elevates the soil level. The plants, plus the levees, have kept this whole area from becoming one big lake, fed by the two largest rivers in California."

Evan left the gravel road for a narrower one, bordered by a canal on one side, and riparian land on the other. Soon a twelve-acre plot of ground appeared. A dock, several rowboats, and a speedboat stood at the dock by the water's edge. The land sloped up to where a group of buildings stood. The crushed-stone driveway, which wound up the slope, was bordered by native sycamore and aspen trees. Poppies, ferns, and purple thyme had sprung up under the trees.

"Breathtaking!" exclaimed Ruth.

"Wait until you see the rest of the place," responded Evan, as he parked his car under the portico of the main building. From the outside, the residence had the appearance of a stucco and stone lodge. Two heavy wooden doors opened into a three-story hall, which led into a lounge, with a beamed ceiling and a stone fireplace rising up at one end of room.   Comfortable sofas were arranged near the fireplace. Chairs with ottomans were next to tables and lamps, encouraging reading or relaxing. A Steinway grand was located opposite the fireplace. A thick thirty-foot Sarouk rug lay on the stone floor.

Evan led Ruth into the adjoining library, which was paneled with alder wood that was native to the area. The shelves were arranged in sections for history, science, nature, religion, and the arts. In addition, one section was devoted to fiction, another to politics and current events.

"Through that doorway," Evan pointed, "are the offices for Reverend Howard, his secretary, and me, the business manager." Turning back into the lounge, Evan took Ruth through sliding doors into a garden. In the middle of the garden was a fountain, surrounded by a curved wooden bench for seating. To the rear of the fountain was a rose garden where yellow, white, and salmon-colored roses intermingled with lavender cyclamen and pink flowering ferns. To the right of the fountain was a lawn on which croquet had been set up; to the left another lawn, where badminton could be played.

Evan escorted Ruth through a trellis gate and into a small octagonal-shaped chapel. "Ooh!" exclaimed Ruth as she entered. The walls and floor were of stone. The sides of the chapel had been built to allow four niches to alternate with four windows, which looked out to Arroyo willow trees. In one of the niches, a wooden shelf held a crucifix and two candleholders. Ferns alternated with statues of angels in the other niches. Folding wooden chairs had been placed on the floor, facing the 'shelf' altar.

"If I worked here," said Ruth. "I would come here every day to meditate."

"I can see you here," said Evan. "A beautiful place for a beautiful girl."

Chapter VI: Reverend Howard

"Well, did you get a better sense of what Evan is really like, after seeing where he lives and works?" asked Mrs. Martin when she and Ruth next visited.

"Somewhat. He knows a lot about nature and seems to enjoy being a part of it, with fishing, boating, and wildlife. He certainly understands the terrain in which he lives."

"What did you think of it, Ruthie?"

"It's idyllic. It's quite remote from the busy, active world, but it's a wonderful place for a retreat."

"Is Evan the 'retreat' type? I can't see a young man who is interested in expensive cars being interested in helping the poor."

"I agree. He's an enigma, but I like him, Mom."

***

Within the next two weeks, Evan told Ruth about an opening for a counseling position at the retirement center. "I know that you are finishing your requirements soon, Ruth," he said. "Why not apply here. I think you would love it, and I would love having you near." Ruth agreed to fill out an application. She sent it in and waited to hear from Evan. Several days later, Evan called to say that he had set up an appointment for Ruth with Reverend Howard.

"I'll drive down to get you," Evan offered. "It's rather a secluded spot to find on your own, and you will want to be relaxed."

"Should I interview with anyone else there?"

"No. If Reverend Howard likes you, he will probably introduce you to the other counselor on board – Peter Paulson."

"What's he like? Has he been there long?"

"Yes, for several years. He's nothing to worry about. He's a *milquetoast.*"

"That's an odd expression."

"You'll see what I mean when you meet him. He's a very bland guy, easy to get along with. Personally, I like a relationship with a little *sizzle* to it."

"O.K." said Ruth. She had no further questions.

***

When they arrived at the center, Evan took Ruth to meet with Reverend Howard, who had found her application interesting. Evan introduced her to the reverend as he came out of his office. Ruth's initial assessment of him was that he was an esthetic-looking man with gray hair and a straight posture. He shook hands and invited Ruth into his office.

"Your resume looks promising," he said. "You're a young ambitious woman, just getting started. However, I'm wondering why you would want to come out here to a secluded area."

"Evan showed me about, and I was thinking that this beautiful, peaceful locale would encourage the residents to meditate and pray. That appeals to me. The founder, Edward Mills, must have been a remarkable man to have had the foresight for a community like this."

"Yes. Let me tell you the history of the center:

"Edward Mills was an investor and vintner who purchased several thousands of acres of land in the delta region about a century ago. He employed hundreds of immigrant workers to tend his vines. As he prospered, he built for his wife Lois and his son Matthew this luxurious three-story mansion. Unfortunately, Matthew died in World War I. Then Matthew's son John died in World War II. In their senior years, Lois and Edward invited a nurse and doctor to live at the mansion to care for them and for other infirm elderly friends who often retreated here. Many of their friends were from Christian churches in the San Joaquin Valley. Other church leaders gradually reached out to Lois and Edward for a retreat center for their congregations. The Forward in Faith Foundation was created to foster the retreat and various other Christian endeavors. Upon Lois' death, Edward had the mansion converted to a retirement center for seniors, established a trust to control the funds, and chose a board of directors."

"He certainly turned his tragedy into a blessing for others," Ruth remarked.

"Indeed. The counselors play a large role in the 'blessings.' They have a close working relationship. We realize that they need time to rejuvenate from their spiritual endeavors; so, each counselor has free time, separate duties, and shared duties. The counselors need to live here. We always have one counselor on duty at all times. Each counselor has their own apartment, which includes a study that can be used for appointments with the residents."

"Any questions or comments, Ruth?"

'Evan showed me around. So; I have seen the common rooms on the first floor, and the garden, patio, and chapel. The chapel is a touch of paradise!"

"Complete with angels," mused Reverend Howard. "Now, if you are interested, I'd like you to meet our other counselor, Peter Paulson, and have him show you around again, this time including the counselor apartments on the second floor."

Peter promptly answered Reverend Howard's call, was introduced to Ruth, and took her first on a tour of the chapel, the garden, and the grounds. Then he escorted her around the first floor of the residence: the lounge area, the formal dining room, the less-formal breakfast room, and the library.

Next, he took her upstairs to see a counselor's apartment. The door to the apartment opened into a small entrance hall containing a coat closet. The living room held a sofa and two chairs, lamps, tables, and a T.V. set. Ruth pictured herself living here and envisioned her Gar Lon Lim painting of the Carmel Mission hanging above the sofa. In the bedroom were a chest of drawers, a queen-sized bed, and a nightstand. She pictured her Marshall Merritt seascape hanging above the bed. Along the wall were two closets with sliding doors. "Plenty of closet space," she observed. A sliding door led to a bath with a toilet, a tub, a separate shower, and a long counter space with a sink, mirror, and drawers. Finally, Peter showed her the study, which was paneled and had a wall of shelves, a desk with a computer, two leather chairs sharing an ottoman, a coffee table, and a lamp table. The window in the study looked out to the dock and the canal.

As Ruth stood at the window, Peter suggested a walk to the dock. They strolled down the driveway to the dock, where ducks and Canadian geese were swimming near the water's edge. Two sandhill cranes waded in a reedy pool nearby.

"Are residents and employees allowed to use these boats?" asked Ruth.

"Yes. There is a sign-up sheet in the secretary's office. However, the center encourages boaters to stay close to the center. This canal is connected to hundreds of other canals, sloughs, streams, and rivers that wind their way on a tortuous path to the Suisun Basin. It would be so easy to get lost."

"Do you go boating or fishing, Peter?"

"Yes, but not as much as Evan. Say, here he comes now!"

Ignoring Peter, Evan hurried up to Ruth, put his arm around her waist, and said, "We'd better get going." Ruth thanked Peter for the tour and started up the driveway towards the car.

"I'll be in touch with you about moving," Peter called to Ruth.

As Evan pulled away, Ruth looked back at Peter, who was still at the dock: he was an average-looking man, average height, average build, average looks but, it seemed to her, a man of pleasing politeness and sensitivity.

"So, you got the job," Evan said.

"Yes. I'll be moving in at the end of next week. I plan to bring my Mini with me."

"You'll never find your way out here alone. I'll drive my car, and you can follow in yours."

"No, your car and mine are too small to carry my large wardrobe, toiletries, boxes of files, DVD player, CD player, and all of my DVDs, CDs, paintings, and photographs; in addition to my coffee maker, ironing board and iron, hairdryer, electric toothbrush, and flosser."

"Ok. OK. I get the point."

"Peter volunteered to drive down in his pick-up and help me to load up, and then I will follow him back here in my Mini."

"A day with plucky Peter Paulson. Lucky you," said Evan with sarcasm.

Chapter VII: Peter

Two weeks later, when Peter drove up and exited his truck, Mrs. Martin happened to be holding Posie, both looking out the window of the lounge. Her initial assessment of Peter was positive: attractive and unassuming. After Ruth had introduced her mother to Peter, they conversed until it was time for the move. Mrs. Martin stood by with Posie as Ruth and Peter loaded all of Ruth's belongings into Peter's pickup and Ruth's Mini. Mrs. Martin liked Peter's handling of himself: pleasant, polite, helpful, and thoughtful. After Ruth had seated herself in the Mini, her mother leaned in the window, smiled, raised her eyebrows, cocked her head in the direction of Peter's pickup, and said, "Bring him again, Ruthie."

When Ruth and Peter arrived at the center, Evan's car stood in the driveway with several packages on the passenger's seat, but Evan was nowhere in sight. Peter helped Ruth carry up to her room her clothing and other belongings. Ruth had left the clothes on hangers and had transported them in the back of her hatchback. It took Peter and Ruth several trips up and down stairs to fetch them and then hang them on the bar in her closet. Ruth directed Peter where to leave her labeled boxes and where to set her two oil paintings and her pictures.

When he had finished, Ruth said, "I have no way to offer you a thank-you cup of coffee."

"No problem," Peter responded. "I'll get us coffee from downstairs, and I'll grab my toolbox and hang your paintings and your pictures so you can begin to feel at home."

"It's dinner time," announced Peter when he finished hanging the last picture.

"Oh, it's been a long day. I'm hungry, but I don't feel up to meeting new people right now, Peter."

"O.K. I'll order food to be brought to us here in the room."

As Peter and Ruth ate from trays, with their legs stretched out on the ottoman, Ruth said, "You've certainly been helpful and welcoming today, Peter."

"Just following Reverend Howard's suggestion."

"What's he like working for?" she asked.

"He's a 'hands off' employer. He gives advice but lets you find your own solutions to problems or situations. He's too busy to be otherwise. In addition to the center, he is the rector of Grace Christian Church in Lodi." Peter took the card for the church out of his billfold and handed it to Ruth.

"Thank you. How does he handle worship services at both places?"

"On Sunday, he preaches in Lodi and locally broadcasts his sermons, which we listen to on television. There are screens located in our lounge and in the dining room for the residents to watch. Then on Wednesday mornings, an informal worship service is held in the lounge. Sometimes I substitute for him when needed."

"Do you answer strictly to Reverend Howard in relation to your duties, Peter, or to Evan as well?"

"Only to the reverend. If I have a financial situation, I go through Edith Moss, his secretary. You'll meet her tomorrow, along with the residents you will be working with. Then you and I will sit down together, and I'll fill you in on their background information."

There was a knock at Ruth's door. As she answered it, she saw Evan standing there. "I've been looking everywhere for you, in the dining room, in the lounge, in the garden. Everywhere. Oh, you have company." Peter arose, nodded at Evan, and said to Ruth, "Meet me at 9:00 in the morning in the library, Ruth."

"O.K. Thanks again for everything, Peter. Goodnight."

"There goes 'perfect Peter,'" quipped Evan. Ruth ignored the remark.

***

In the library the following morning, Peter explained to Ruth that they were both responsible for the communal welfare of the residents in informal situations. Regarding counseling, the female residents would be directed to Ruth for appointments and the male to Peter.

"You will interact with each individual for her counseling needs and then with a group of residents that we call 'the circle.' Each Monday at 1:00 p.m., circle sessions are held in the library."

"Why are they called 'circle' sessions?" Ruth asked.

"Because we sit in a circle so that each person can see and interact with all of the others."

"What is the purpose of the circle sessions?" she asked.

"To counteract loneliness and encourage reaching out to others. Religiously speaking, to learn to 'love your neighbor as yourself.'"

"Isn't that rather impossible for human beings?"

"It's impossible to achieve, but worth aiming for."

"Will we each have our own circle to be responsible for?" asked Ruth.

"No. The men and the women meet together during our group meetings. The male-female interaction is important to a healthy spiritual life. Actually, Ruth, we have only ten permanent residents at the center. A lot of the people are temporary residents, who are here for a retreat, either alone or with a church group."

"So, you and I are both leaders of the circle," said Ruth.

"Yes. We will share that duty. Each will attend the sessions, but we will alternate taking the leadership role. I will be taking the leadership during the first session to acquaint you with the process."

Peter looked at his watch. "It's lunchtime," he announced. "Let's go into the dining room to eat. Most of the circle will be there, and I'll briefly introduce you to each of them. Then this afternoon, we can meet about 2:00 p.m. in my office, and I will share background information about the residents."

In the dining room, the circle group were sitting at three separate tables: at one table, were a distinguished-looking man and three women; at another, two men; at a third table, a woman sat alone, reading a book while she ate. Peter and Ruth joined them before taking their food out to the garden to continue their visit.

During a break before meeting again with Peter, Ruth took a walk down to the dock. Evan was just returning. "What did the *illustrious Mr. Paulson* have in store for you this morning?" he asked Ruth.

"He took me around to meet the circle discussion group."

"So-o-o-o, what did you think of Gloria?"

"Gloria who?"

"Gloria Lancaster, the best-looking woman in the group."

"Lancaster?"

"Yes, my grandmother."

"Why didn't you introduce her to me when you first showed me around, Evan?" asked Ruth. He shrugged.

"Gloria doesn't need an introduction," he said. "She makes herself known."

Chapter VIII: The Circle

When Ruth entered Peter's study, he handed her a binder with dividers and notebook paper and offered her one of his ballpoint pens. Lifting his own binder from his desk, he said, "I'm going to give to you background information on each of the residents in the circle group, in alphabetical order. Feel free to ask questions, make comments, and jot down notes. Also, I will give you a picture of each person for your binder."

The first picture was that of Ralph Baldwin. Ruth recognized him as one of the two men sitting together in the dining room. He was a white, well-dressed, partly bald man of average height and weight. Peter described him as a seventy-five-year-old wealthy retired investor who had traveled to different geographical and cultural areas. "His wife is deceased," Peter said. "Their son Brooks lives nearby; he is a friend of Evan Lancaster."

The second picture was that of Cynthia Denton, a seventy-year-old woman of average height and weight, with gray hair styled in a pixie cut, and a pleasant expression. Peter described Cindy as a retired primary school teacher, who is widowed and has two daughters and five grandchildren. "She is interested in movies, mystery books, crafts and games," he added.

The third was that of Judy Hastings, an eighty-year-old woman with white coiffed hair. Peter described her as average in height and weight. Being a housewife was her career. After her husband died, she named their son Jacob as the trustee of their large estate. Peter said, "She is very proud of Jacob and spends a lot of time with him and his family. Her interests have been the same throughout her lifetime: charities, cuisine, decorating, news, and music."

"This is Gloria Lancaster," Peter remarked as he handed Ruth Gloria's picture. "She is eighty-one years old, but she looks younger. She is a former model." The picture was that of a regal-looking, tall, slender, fashionably dressed woman. "Her husband, Roger, and her son, Morgan, are deceased. Her grandson, Evan, is the trustee of her estate. She is interested in fashion, art, music, antiques, gardening, and the environment," said Peter.

"Next is Elisabeth Lim," he continued. He handed Ruth a picture of a tiny eighty-two-year-old Asian female, with white hair, styled in a bun. "Ms. Lim is a retired college professor of literature, a maiden lady with no living relatives. She is interested in studying, analyzing, and discussing literature, history, religion, psychology, and science." Ruth recognized her as the woman seated alone in the dining room.

The fifth picture was that of Oscar Oliver, a seventy-nine-year-old Hispanic male with gray hair. He was tall and portly, dressed jauntily, and appeared nonchalant. Peter described him as "a retired wealthy realtor who is interested in property, investments, and the geography of California, particularly, the delta. He is a widower and has one estranged son, named Jake, who is also a friend of Evan."

The last picture was that of Dr. Luke Sandler, a seventy-eight-year-old Caucasian male, who was tall and slender, with a sober appearance. "Dr. Luke is a retired internist," Peter informed Ruth. "He is a bachelor and has no living relatives. Naturally, he is interested in medicine, as well as science, religion, psychology, art, and music."

"Do you have any questions, Ruth?" Peter asked.

"Do these people like each other?" she inquired.

"Some more than others. Our job as counselors is to promote their individual welfare and to help them to understand and appreciate the welfare of others. So; private individual counseling and interaction within the discussion group are the methods we use."

"Who chooses the topics for discussion?" Ruth asked.

"You and I do. Personally, I have a broad direction that I plan to take, but I also ask residents for topics that they have wondered about or areas of doubt which they would like to discuss. If you need help with spiritual guidance or enlightenment, you can come to me or go to Reverend Howard. He is a very knowledgeable, Christ-centered man."

"Will you help me to get started with preparation to lead the group?" asked Ruth.

"Of course. The next session is at 1:00 p.m. on Monday. I will be leading it, and you may observe and watch my technique, which you may adopt or not, as you choose. In the meantime, I'll loan you several books that I found helpful when I first became a leader."

"Thanks, Peter. I'd like to go to the chapel now until dinner. May I?"

"You never need to ask for permission to go to the chapel, Ruth. Go and meditate. You've had a lot to assimilate today."

Chapter IX: Angels

When Ruth entered the library for the meeting on Monday, the group was already assembled. Peter had set up an extra folding chair in the circle for her. He introduced her and then named each resident around the circle.

"Ruth Martin is here to observe," Peter informed them. "Ruth and I will take turns leading the discussion after today." The group clapped politely. Peter said, "The subject today is the existence of angels. Do angels exist? If so, are there good and bad angels? What is their mission?" He paused, then addressed Elizabeth. "Do angels exist?"

"I've never felt the presence of an angel, but angels are mentioned in the scriptures," she answered.

"Yes," Judy continued. "There is the story of an angel announcing to Mary that she will bear a son."

"Yes, the story of the angel Gabriel," explained Elizabeth. "Gabriel appeared first to Zacharius, the husband of Mary's cousin, Elizabeth. Elizabeth was too old to conceive and bear children. But she conceived a son by the Holy Spirit, who became John, the Baptist, the forerunner of Christ. The angel next appeared to Mary and announced to her that she had been chosen by God to conceive Christ, through the power of the Holy Spirit."

"That's correct," acknowledged Peter. "In both cases, the mission of Gabriel was to deliver a message from God."

"The immaculate conception has always been difficult for me to believe," remarked Ralph Baldwin.

"Me, too," agreed Oscar Oliver. "It kind of turns males into useless creatures."

"From a scientific point of view, what do you think, Dr. Sandler?" Peter asked.

"Well, the male is not needed for some species to survive. There is one female spider who produces hundreds of baby spiders within her body without interaction with a male. God created that species; so; that ability exists in nature. Besides, we are told that 'all things are possible through God.'"

Cindy Denton shuddered. "Ugh! Hundreds of baby spiders crawling everywhere!"

"How do you visualize angels, Cindy?" Peter asked.

"As they are often portrayed in the art world: cute, chubby, little Cherubims and majestic Seraphims with big wings."

"I see angels appearing in choirs to praise and adore, like the angels appearing to the shepherds in the field at the time of the birth of Jesus," commented Gloria Lancaster.

"As heavenly creatures praising God with harps and voices," described Ralph. "Visit the Sistine Chapel in Italy, and you'll see how angels were portrayed by Michelangelo."

"I see them having different characteristics," said Dr. Sandler. "Some are like the archangel Michael, a fearsome, powerful being with a booming voice, descending from heaven with Christ on Judgement Day. Others can be fearsome, but docile, like the angels appearing in shining garments in the tomb of the missing, risen Christ."

"You are all portraying only the good angels," suggested Elizabeth. "The Bible does not include God's creation of the angels; but the epic poem, *Paradise Lost*, devotes an entire section to how the created angels broke into the factions of good and evil: those who praised and adored God and those who envied God and turned against Him. God kept the good angels in His heavenly realm and expelled the bad into the realm of darkness. Out of hatred for God, the devil and his followers were determined to destroy God's creation."

Peter explained that although "Genesis" does not give a description of the bad angels, including the creation of man, the penultimate book of "Jude" in the Bible states that some of the angels did not keep the position for which they were created, to praise and glorify God; and therefore, they were expelled from Heaven and thrown into darkness.

Gloria said, "It bothers me that there is no explanation for the creation of evil in our world. It must have started somewhere."

Dr. Sandler answered. "The human mind can't completely understand the spiritual. So, I look for a parallel to the spiritual in a human form. A healthy tree can survive and even flourish with a withered branch, and when the withered branch is cut off, only the good remains. I think that God created only what was good, and evil grew out of the good. As earthly creatures, we cannot see God's purpose."

"Well put," Peter said, "We will be delving more into the topic of good vs. evil in our sessions coming up. Let's end in prayer."

When the residents had left the library, Peter invited Ruth to join him for coffee in the garden. Ruth opened the dialogue.

"Your handling of the discussion today and your knowledge of scripture suggest that you've had a background in theology."

"Seminary for two years," he answered.

"Tell me a little about yourself, Peter."

"I grew up in Tucson, Arizona. I attended Tucson Public Schools and then the University of Arizona, majoring in psychology. Following graduation, I entered St. Paul's Seminary at Berkeley. I left after two years because I decided that the priesthood was not for me. I looked around for a job as a Christian therapist, interviewed with Reverend Howard, and here I am."

"Do you have family in Tucson?"

"Yes, my parents and two brothers. My older brother is a history professor at the U of A, and my younger brother is a lieutenant in the army, stationed in San Antonio, Texas."

"Is either of them married, with kids?"

"Both of them. I'm an uncle four times over. How about you, Ruth?"

"No siblings. No plans for marriage."

Raising his coffee cup, Peter said, "To what lies ahead for you, Ruth."

Chapter X: Peter and Evan

Peter and Ruth were meeting in his office to discuss the circle session of the previous day.

"Did you have any feedback from the residents about our discussion yesterday?" Peter asked.

"No. I don't think that the residents know me well enough yet for that."

"Perhaps," agreed Peter. "Cindy Denton came to me afterwards about Elizabeth Lim. She feels that Elizabeth treats her like a school girl."

"I could see that Elizabeth enjoyed sharing her knowledge, perhaps coming across as a lecturer."

Peter responded, "That's exactly what she spent her life doing: seeking and analyzing knowledge and then relaying it to others; whereas, Cindy has devoted her life to making her husband, daughters, and grandchildren happy. Now that her husband is deceased, she sometimes feels unneeded."

"What did you say to Cindy?" asked Ruth.

"I explained that Elizabeth has filled her life with information from books. 'You are the fortunate one, Cindy,' I reminded her. 'You have had a life of loving and being loved. Elizabeth tends to lecture all of us when it comes to books, but she is the most well-read, and we can learn from her study of classical literature.' I added that one of my favorite books is James Harriott's *All Creatures Great and Small,* which is not classical literature but a collection of human-interest stories. "Have you read it, Ruth?"

"Yes. It's delightful. Great insights about people and nature. What was Cindy's response?"

"She seemed satisfied and then asked me if I had a copy of the Harriott book, which I did, and I loaned it to her."

"Thanks for sharing that with me, Peter. It gives me an insight into understanding both Elizabeth and Cindy. By the way, to date, I've had no requests for appointments with any of the female residents."

"You will soon. This week, however, you will want to devote yourself to preparation for the next circle session. I was thinking of continuing the topic of good and evil with a discussion about devils or demons, the bad angels. Would you be willing to do that?"

"Yes. Since we just discussed the good angels, it is logical to discuss the bad angels; however, I don't know much about devils or demons."

"I have some excellent study and reading material by renowned historians, clergy, and theologians that I can loan to you. Also, our library is a good source for research."

"O.K. I'll get started by reading and taking notes."

Ruth spent the afternoon in the library. She looked through the card catalogue by words relating to the topic, then collected books from shelves, skimmed through them, selected those she wished to read, and began taking notes. By 5:00 p.m., she needed a break.

She walked down to the dock and sat on a wooden bench located at the edge of the water, where she could watch the waterfowl. Several ducks, searching for food, were diving in and out of sponge plants, with their green pods and white blossoms. A cute river otter swam nearby on its way to the reeds growing near the opposite bank. The sound of a motorboat preceded the sight of Evan and a young man unfamiliar to Ruth.

Evan docked the boat and then introduced his companion as Jake Oliver, Oscar's son. Jake was about Ruth's age, but he had the appearance of a grimy, weather-beaten fisherman. With him was a black water spaniel. The two men did not appear that they had been fishing. There was no sign of rods, net, or a string of fish.

"No fish, I see," commented Ruth.

"No, we explored a few islands and waterways today," answered Evan. "Did you know that there are fifty-two major islands to explore in the seven hundred miles of waterways?"

"Gosh!" Ruth exclaimed. "Do they all have names?"

"Many of the smaller ones don't. The three largest are Decker Island, Bethel Island, and Brannon Island, the closest one to here."

"And then there are Tyler, Prospect, Sutter, and Andrus," added Jake.

"Have you been to all of them?" Ruth asked Jake.

"No," he answered, "but I intend to."

A life of leisure in the delta, Ruth surmised. "Do you find time for a job?"

"I run an animal shelter that Evan and I started in Sacramento, on land owned by my dad. Seebee, here, is a shelter dog," he said, pointing.

"Lucky you," Ruth responded as she got up to leave. "Nice meeting you, Jake. Lovely water spaniel!"

***

Ruth spent the rest of the week in the library, where she could quickly consult a reference book. She continued to read and take notes until she was ready to begin an outline and compose possible questions for the session on Monday. She was resting in the chapel early on Friday evening when Peter approached her.

"Getting refilled?" he asked. She nodded. "Ruth, you've worked hard on a difficult topic. It is spiritually exhausting to concentrate on evil for an extended period of time. Why don't you go home to Los Gatos for the weekend, where you'll be surrounded by beauty and serenity? When you come back, I'll be with you on Monday to lend you support."

"Thanks, Evan. I'll leave early in the morning."

***

When Ruth arrived home, she found her mother in the garden, deadheading the roses, while Posie nosed around in a bed of garlic and herbs. Posie barked, ran to Ruth, and jumped into her arms. She cuddled Posie and buried her face in Posie's fur. "Mm," she said, "You smell like pizza, Posie." Mrs. Martin looked up, laid her clippers down, and gave her daughter a hug.

"You look hot and tired, Ruthie. Why don't you change into a swimsuit and take a dip in the pool while I prepare lunch for us? We can eat on the patio." The previous day, Mrs. Martin had prepared a Quiche Lorraine. She brought it out to the patio, along with a tossed salad and a bowl of fruit. At the wrought iron table, Ruth chose a chair that faced a corner of the garden where a birdbath, flanked by stone replicas of the *Los Gatos cats,* stood underneath a broad magnolia tree, with large, glossy leaves and white blossoms.

"I miss that tree," Ruth said to her mother.

"Dad and I miss having **you** around, Ruthie."

During their visit, Mrs. Martin encouraged Ruth to describe her new life: the locale, the center, the apartment, the staff, and the residents. Ruth's description was largely positive. Her mother was not surprised. Ruth had been raised to look for the good, to be appreciative, and to care about others. She was sure that Ruth would be successful in her chosen career. However, she knew that Ruth was tender-hearted, and she did not want to see her taken advantage of.

"Do you see much of Evan at the center?" she asked.

"Usually in the dining room or in the garden. Yesterday, I saw him at the dock, coming back from boating with a friend of his, kind of a scruffy-looking guy with a shelter dog."

"Did he introduce you to his friend?"

"Yes, he is the son of one of the residents. He told me that Evan and he own a shelter for dogs and cats in Sacramento."

"A mission for the poor in Oakland and a shelter for animals in Sacramento? Evan is quite a do-gooder, it appears." She paused. "And how is Peter, the nice young man who helped you move?"

"He is pleasant to work with. We see a lot of each other because of our jobs. Actually, I think that Evan may be jealous of him. If Evan sees Peter and me talking, he comes over to us and butts into our conversation or puts his arm around me and leads me away."

"Don't let yourself be led by him, Ruthie. Possessiveness does not end well."

Chapter XI: Demons

Ruth, Peter, and the circle group gathered in the library. Ruth began the discussion: "Our topic today is the existence of devils, demons, and evil spirits. In the Christian religion, the devil is considered the source of all evil. In 'Genesis 3' of the Bible, the serpent seduces Eve to bring sin and rebellion into Paradise. 'Genesis' does not explain how the devil came into being. However, in the 17th century, John Milton wrote a detailed literary account of the devil's fall from Heaven in his epic poem, *Paradise Lost*. Elizabeth, you've taught *Paradise Lost*. Will you give us a brief synopsis of Book I?"

"Gladly," responded Elizabeth: "God created the angels before humans. He gave them a hierarchical order of powers – archangels, seraphims, cherubims, etc., and assigned them duties. Lucifer, one of the most powerful of the angels, became enraged when God gave His only begotten Son power over Lucifer. Lucifer persuaded a group of angels to join him in waging war against God and the obedient angels. God expelled Lucifer and his followers from Heaven and into darkness. Out of revenge, the fallen angels devoted themselves to destroying God's creation, including mankind."

"Thank you, Elizabeth. In the Bible, evil is introduced as a serpent, who personifies evil, and God personifies goodness. Belief in the existence of evil is not just Biblical. History, anthropology, religion, literature, and sociology all confirm that evil exists. Almost all cultures have believed in a destructive source of evil that creates havoc in the world and wishes to destroy mankind.

"The Bible calls the evil spirit by different names: **the serpent** or **Satan** or **The Prince of the World**. What other names have you heard or read about that personify evil?"

When no one answered, Elizabeth recited: "**The Prince of Darkness, the Prince of the Air, Lucifer, Mammon, Beelzebub,**

Moloch, Beliel, Asmodeus." Oscar looked at Ralph and lifted his eyebrows at this list.

"There are a lot of common names for the devil, too: **the tempter, the deceiver, the enemy, the liar**," said Judy.

"Throughout the ages, people have feared different forms of evil," added Gloria. "Monsters, ghouls, ghosts, apparitions, dead souls, things that go bump in the night."

Ruth pointed out that atheists often scoff at this fear, believing that it stems from ignorance and shows an infantile stage of human development. Ralph exclaimed, "They're the ignorant ones."

"From my research," continued Ruth, "I learned that 70% of U.S. citizens believe in the existence of evil spirits and 50% believe that evil spirits actively disrupt harmony in the world and sometimes even attempt to take possession of humans."

Dr. Sandler entered the discourse: "There is a growing belief in parapsychology today. Rather than seeking knowledge from the traditional fields of religion and psychology, some people are turning to mediums and healers to find physical evidence of the spiritual world. That is an impossibility and can lead to deception."

"Can you give us an example of that from your experience as a doctor?" asked Ruth.

"A schizophrenic, for example, could have genetic reasons for hearing voices or seeing non-existent people and should be helped with medication; whereas a histrionic individual may just be play-acting for attention and needs to be counseled and not medicated. Unfortunately, if the person seeks help from a charlatan, who is only seeking money or fame, he will be taken advantage of, often with severe consequences."

Ruth said, "Charlatans often try to confuse their victim, putting themselves and the victim in the hands of the devil, who is a great deceiver. The devil's deception can be insidious. He can begin tempting a victim into committing a teeny, weeny, insignificant sin, which can grow into a horrendous sin. Can you think of an example of that in the Bible?"

Gloria responded. "The story of King David. His sin begins by his desire for Bathsheba, whom he sees bathing on her rooftop. He sends her husband Uriel into the front lines of a battle, where he is killed. So, in the end, David is guilty of committing murder."

"Thank you, Gloria." Ruth continued. "Another characteristic of the devil is his ability to feign goodness, for example, by sending a false message to his victim. The message may come through a dream in which the victim is told that he is to undertake an important mission in the world, such as warning others about the end of the world. Since God has used dreams to convey messages, these false messages can be interpreted as coming from God."

Elizabeth spoke up authoritatively, "It's so foolish to fall for that. Demons **cannot know** the end. God created the beginning, and **only God can know when it will end**."

"Well," said Ruth, "I'm sure you've all experienced having dreams that you couldn't understand." Everyone nodded. "Have you ever tried to interpret a dream or to ask someone else to interpret it?"

"I dreamt that I would soon meet the love of my life," said Oscar.

"You're still dreaming, Oscar," quipped Ralph. Amid laughter, Ruth said, "Moving on, another characteristic of the devil is that he is multi-talented; he knows how to tempt man into many types of sin. I've made a list of sins and grouped them. Please feel free to add to this list as I go through it. First, the sins that civilized societies deem unlawful: stealing, defrauding, violence against others (Ralph added: murder, rape, abduction, incest); second, sins that are not unlawful but are deemed socially wrong or immoral, such as hatred, jealousy, rage (Cindy added: belittling or degrading others; Judy added:

revenge, callousness, self-centeredness, self-indulgence); third, sins attacking God, such as railing against God, poking fun at believers, attempting to turn others from God, ignoring God (Dr. Sandler added: replacing love for God with a love of money or achievement or power, or love of self.)

Peter entered the discussion at this point. "It's normal for people to attempt to characterize some sins as more atrocious than others, but they are all a rebellion against God. However, I feel that some are more consequential to the sinner than others. For instance, the closing of one's mind to the Holy Spirit can result in spiritual death. If the Holy Spirit tries over and over to speak to you and you do not listen, God eventually will say, 'Well, then, **thy** will be done. And you will have eternal separation from God.'"

"Let's let that thought sink in," said Ruth; she paused briefly before continuing. "The final attribute of the devil I wish to discuss today is the devil's possessiveness, which is an **extremely dangerous** quality. In researching for our topic today, I read a book entitled *Demonic Foes* by Richard Gallagher, a psychiatrist who has worked with clients suffering from possession by the devil. I have taken the facts of one case and put them into a narrative that I will share with you. Listen, please:

'As a teenager, John was curious about the spiritual world. Light-heartedly, he sought information from a Ouija Board, tried concocting potions, used incantations, and delved into other occult acts. Nothing bad happened to him. He matured into a sensible, thoughtful, God-fearing young man.

At one stage of his adult life, he was very lonely, depressed, and vulnerable. The devil pounced. First, he attacked John's senses. John became plagued with strange noises and voices and with objects breaking or moving about. He began seeing ghosts and shadows. Then his body was attacked. He had unexplained bruises and scratches. Next, his mind was assaulted. He would go into a trance-like state, with no memory of it later. John sought the help of a medical doctor and then a psychiatrist, but they could find no basis for his suffering. Then he went to a minister who diagnosed his condition as spiritual. The minister encouraged John to study scripture and to pray, and he helped John to do that.

However, the devil became more possessive. He gave John the powers of remote viewing and hidden knowledge (i.e., the ability to see someone who was not within eyesight or the ability to know about someone else's life without any access to that knowledge.) Also, at times, the devil gave him the ability to speak in foreign languages without John's having learned them.

Finally, John sought the help of a team of experts: a psychiatrist, two priests, and an exorcist. On occasions, when there was an attempt to drive out the evil spirit, the devil gave John the ability to levitate and endowed him with inhuman strength. Many attempts were made by the experts to help John, but the devil did not go easily. John needed to continue to follow their spiritual guidance and to apply himself to a regimen of prayer and study of scripture.'

"Dr. Gallagher, who worked with this client, stated that possession of an individual by the devil is rare, but that groups of devil worshippers exist, which are extremely dangerous."

Ralph was the first to speak. "The story of John sounds like the movie, *The Exorcist*."

"It's too fantastic to be realistic," said Judy.

"Creepy!" exclaimed Cindy.

"Does that really happen today?" asked Gloria.

Elizabeth spoke again: "Whatever happened yesterday can happen today. Is the world less evil today? I don't think so. We have more knowledge today and a better understanding of mankind, but we are mortal beings, and we can't completely understand spiritual beings, either good or bad ones."

47

"Yes," agreed Ruth, "and it is dangerous to try to understand the devil. The devil is more powerful and cleverer than humans. We are not on an equal playing field with him."

At this point, Peter again entered the conversation. "Only Jesus has been able to command the devil to lose his hold on a person. The four gospels include seven episodes about demons who possessed victims. Jesus commanded them each in a simple, straightforward, authoritative manner. He had the *power* to do that. The charlatans today who purport to being exorcists use dramatic, complicated techniques, making themselves *look* powerful."

"There are a few capable exorcists today," added Dr. Sandler, "but they work in conjunction with a team because the devil is so powerful."

Peter added, "The International Association of Exorcists was founded in the 1990s. They consult with clergy, doctors, and psychiatrists as advisors about diabolic possession, and they train exorcists; but they can do nothing for an individual if he/she doesn't spiritually fight against the evil."

Ruth asked the group, "Do you have any questions or comments pertaining to today's discussion?"

Elizabeth spoke again. "C.S. Lewis, the famed author and theologian, wrote a novel called the *Screwtape Letters*, in which the two central characters were devils. He admitted later that the project had left him spiritually troubled, and he never again gave the devil central stage; instead, he concentrated on giving God the primary role, such as Aslan, the lion in The Narnia series, which introduced many children and adults to Christ."

Oscar impishly smiled and said, "This whole discussion today reminds me of what my mother used to say: 'Don't let the devil in the door, Oscar. He'll soon take over the house.'" Everyone, except Elizabeth, laughed.

Smiling, Ruth asked Peter to give a closing statement. Peter responded, "The devil is a spiritual being with great power and cunning, but he is revolting against God, who is the **source of *all* power**; so, in the end, the devil cannot win the battle of good versus evil. As believers, we have God on our side."

Chapter XII: Sacramento

Ruth and Peter walked together through the garden, heading for the chapel. "Look how beautiful the roses are today," Peter commented.

"And listen to the birds and the fountain," responded Ruth.

"A touch of Paradise," remarked Peter.

In the chapel, they seated themselves in a spot where the light was streaming through a window, catching motes of dust. Peter began the conversation. "You were well prepared for the discussion today, Ruth."

"Thanks. I appreciated your theological input, Peter. At times today, our discussion focused so much on temptation and evil, but in your closing remarks, you assured us of God's goodness and His power over the devil."

"After Elizabeth's remark about *The Screwtape Letters*, I felt concerned that I had given you a spiritually dangerous topic to pursue, Ruth."

"Don't be concerned. I knew that I could come to you if I began to feel uneasy about my research."

"Thank you, Ruth. I am fortunate to have you working beside me. Now, as we look forward to the next discussion, I feel that we should look at the language of 'Genesis,' particularly from a literary point of view. The text is not written in a language used by a historian but more in the style of a poet. The poet or poets give the reader a broad timeline of God's creation of the world."

"The book of 'Genesis' is long. How many chapters do you think we should cover?" Ruth asked Peter.

"Three: Chapters one and two, describing that God created what was good, and Chapter three, which describes the entering of evil into his Paradise. The 'good' story has to come first, but if you prepare for that, Ruth, you won't have a break in your work schedule; however, if you take the 'evil' story, it puts you back into centering on evil."

"Since I have a lot of material I've collected on 'evil', I could use some of that; so, I'll stick with that. Afterall, I have **you** to give me support, Peter."

"Thanks, Ruth, for your willingness. Let's check bases again before and after the next session." He looked at his watch. "I have an appointment, but stay, Ruth, and enjoy the chapel."

***

When Ruth walked back through the garden, Evan was playing croquet with Brooks Baldwin, Ralph's son. When Evan saw Ruth, he put down his mallet, walked over to Ruth, and took her by the arm. "Save me from Brooks," he whispered to her.

"Why?"

"Brooks is a spoiled brat; he acts up if I knock his ball out of bounds, and he cheats if I don't watch him like a hawk."

"Why do you play with him?"

"Because his father is wealthy, and Brooks is the trustee of Ralph's estate."

"What difference does that make to you?"

"I'm always looking for donations for my mission in Oakland and my animal shelter in Sacramento. Also, I'm in charge of finance for the Forward in Faith Foundation and the Treasurer here at the center. Everything requires money for operation, Ruth."

"Of course," said Ruth. "Perhaps you should approach Ralph instead of Brooks."

"I don't think so. Brooks describes his father as a skinflint, who wants to hang onto his money."

Ruth didn't want to discuss Ralph with Evan, so she changed the topic: "Did you go fishing this week, Evan?"

"No. I haven't been since you saw me with Jake Oliver at the boat dock. That reminds me, I have to go to Sacramento on Saturday to see Jake about business at the animal shelter. Why not come with me? I'll show you the shelter, and afterwards we can have some fun in Sacramento."

"O.K. I need an outing."

***

On Saturday, Ruth met Evan in the lobby. She was dressed in slacks, a blouse, and sneakers and was carrying a light khaki jacket. Evan took hold of the jacket and said, "You should bring a warmer jacket; we're going out on the water later. You might want to rethink the scarf, too."

Ruth felt miffed. She had grown up in California and knew that the heat of the day would give way to a chill in the evening. And she knew how the wind and water could affect the temperature. Rather than arguing with him, she went up to her apartment to select a warmer jacket. As she glanced in the mirror, her lovely sea green scarf complimented her auburn hair. *Dammit*, she thought, *I'm wearing the scarf*.

As Evan drove along the canal towards the highway, he pointed to the vegetation: the clumps of wild grasses and the red, orange, and white poppies amid the firecracker bushes that had sprung up alongside the gravel road.

"What are those shrubs with long, fleshy sprays of brilliant red-orange flowers?" asked Ruth.

"They're called firecracker plants, probably because of their color," he answered. "They and the poppies grow wild here. By the way, the poppy is the state flower."

"Yes," she answered. "And the mocking bird is the state bird. I learned that in the third grade, Evan."

He smiled. "There aren't any mocking birds in the delta," he stated.

"I'm not surprised," she said. "They prefer the weather in Los Gatos."

On the outskirts of Sacramento, Evan pulled onto a gravel road that led to the entrance of an acreage on which a wooden structure stood, surrounded by a wire fence. The E & J Pet Shelter consisted of a small waiting room, living quarters for Jake Oliver, the manager, and two separate rooms with cages, one for dogs, and one for cats.

"The cages are unlocked, Ruth. Feel free to acquaint yourself with any of the animals while Jake and I attend to business," Evan said.

Ruth spent time with a mature dachshund and then with a beagle puppy. When Evan returned, she was cuddling with a caramel-colored kitten who was burrowing his tiny nails into her neck scarf. Evan scolded her, "The kitten will ruin your scarf, Ruth. I warned you not to wear it."

"No," she countered. "You advised me to rethink the scarf, which I did."

Back in the car, Evan turned on the radio and had nothing to say until they neared the I Street Bridge. Then he informed Ruth that the bridge had been built a century ago, in 1911. "It is what they call a swing bridge," he said.

"What is a swing bridge?" she asked.

"It is a bridge that is built to pivot, with the central section moving to the side, allowing tall ships to pass under it and then moving back into place for traffic over the bridge."

"It must have strong supports on the sides," said Ruth.

"Yes, the triangular position of the metal trusses adds strength, besides being architecturally attractive."

Evan drove into Old Sacramento and parked, and they began walking. Ruth said, "My parents brought me here when I was in elementary school. I remember the old wooden structures with their upper and lower porches, and the plank sidewalks. Oh, look, there's the statue of the pony express rider!"

Evan informed her that Sacramento was the end of the line for a rider bringing mail west from St. Joseph, Missouri. "Actually," he said, "the Pony Express service lasted only for a short period during the Civil War, but it later became romanticized in stories and movies. After only eighteen months, its service was replaced by the telegraph."

Catching sight of a horse and carriage, Evan suggested a carriage ride around Old Sacramento. He named several buildings along the way: the Hastings Building, once the headquarters of the Pony Express; the Lady Adams Building, the oldest of the buildings, built in 1852; the early California Supreme Court Building, the Eagle Theater, and the Transcontinental Railroad Building.

"These buildings have been reconstructed or rebuilt since the days of the forty-niners," Evan informed Ruth. "Sacramento has suffered severe damage from flooding throughout the years because the two major rivers, the Sacramento River and the American River, become swollen from the melting snow in the mountains."

"Have you been to the source of the Sacramento River, Evan?" He shook his head no. Ruth continued. "It starts in the Klamath Mountains and then flows in and out of Lake Shasta before flowing past Sacramento. My parents and I have vacationed on Lake Shasta, and also in the Sierra Nevada Mountains near Lake Tahoe." Evan ceased being a tour guide for the rest of the carriage ride. When it ended, he suggested that they stroll over to the ticket office to purchase tickets for a cruise on the Sacramento River.

The weather on the boat was pleasant – sunny with a slight breeze. Ruth did not need her heavy jacket. The riverboat took them past Old Sacramento and under the I Street Bridge. "The towers of the bridge are 160' in height," said Evan. "It is a lift bridge, so-called because it is divided into sections, which lift vertically, enabling a tall ship to pass underneath. A mechanism raises the sections and then returns them to their horizontal position for cars and trucks."

"With the sun on the bridge today, its gold color is shining. Perhaps the bridge was painted gold to symbolize the forty-niners digging for gold," suggested Ruth.

"Perhaps," agreed Evan. He glanced at his watch. "It's time. Next stop, the Delta King for dinner." The large five-story sternwheel steamboat hotel was just a stone's throw away. Evan resumed his role as tour guide: "Originally christened in 1927, the Delta King traveled daily between Sacramento and San Francisco until 1940, as both a hotel and a means of transportation. Because of severe flooding and then sinking, it was abandoned. It lay partly submerged until the 1980s when a private investor began to restore it as a business venture. It was reopened as a floating hotel in 1989 after the expenditure of nine million dollars."

As Evan and Ruth toured the boat, they could see the evidence of the owner's outlay of money in the plush carpets, etched glass windows, ornate brass fixtures, mahogany woodwork, antique furnishings, and artwork. The restaurant, where they had dinner on board, had marvelous views of the river, bridges, and the waterfront. During dinner, Evan lifted his wine glass to Ruth and said, "To the Delta Queen who sits on board the Delta King tonight."

"To the tour guide," she responded. "Did you know that the real Delta Queen, the twin of the Delta King, is alive and still functioning as a riverboat and hotel on the Ohio and Mississippi Rivers?"

"No, I didn't know that. How did they get her there?"

"They towed her down the west coast of Central America and South America, through the Panama Canal, up the east coast of South America and Central America, into the Gulf of Mexico and up into the Mississippi River. My parents and I sailed on her when we vacationed in New Orleans."

"Well, la-de-da!"

Evan chose to listen to the radio on the way back to the center, and Ruth was left to her own thoughts about the day. It had been an interesting day. She had learned a lot about the area and the history of Sacramento. However, she had found Evan a bit bossy and almost too full of details. She wondered if he had memorized facts to impress her.

Chapter XIII: Gloria and Evan

On Sunday morning, Ruth went into the dining room to have coffee and to listen to Reverend Howard's sermon. She joined a table where Dr. Sandler, Peter, and Gloria were seated. Reverend Howard's topic for the sermon was the story of the Tower of Babel, found in Genesis, Chapter 11. (Babylon, located in present-day Iraq, was inhabited by the descendants of Ham, one of the three sons of Noah, who settled in the area for many generations following the Great Flood.) The Babylonians had developed into a society that was proud of its material achievements. Reverend Howard drew a comparison between Babylonian society and our society today. Like the Babylonians, we still seek to ignore, replace, or rebel against God when we devote our lives to being the richest, the best, or the most powerful.

Following the sermon, the four remained seated at the table to discuss the sermon. In the middle of the discussion, Evan came into the room and walked over to their table. Gloria jokingly said, "Look! A Babylonian has just appeared."

"What do you mean, Gloria?" Evan asked.

"Read Chapter 11 of 'Genesis,'" she responded.

Evan shrugged and turned to Ruth. "I have a photo for you," he said, handing it to her. It was a picture of Evan and Ruth standing in front of the Delta King. Evan had his arm around her waist, and Ruth was smiling at him. As Ruth started to study it, Evan took it from her and handed it to his grandmother.

"Ruth and I spent the day together, Gloria," he explained. Gloria nodded pleasantly at Ruth and passed it on to Dr. Sandler and Peter, who handed it back to Ruth. Dr. Sandler said, "Please excuse me. It is time for me to exercise." Peter also excused himself and left the dining room.

"What are your plans for the day, Evan?" asked Gloria. He explained that he was driving to Santa Cruz to have lunch with a friend.

"It's been a while since you've had lunch with **me**, Evan," Gloria reminded him.

"This is important," he responded. Then kissing Gloria quickly on the cheek and touching Ruth's shoulder, he left.

"That's the Evan of today – a very busy young man," Gloria remarked. "Sometimes I'm proud of him, and sometimes I wonder what he is all about."

"What was he like as a child?" Ruth asked.

"A very sweet, sensitive boy. He was very close to his mother."

"What was she like?"

"Beautiful. Evan has Evangeline's good looks. However, she seldom looked cheerful. My son, Morgan, was a naval captain, and Evangeline and Evan were left at home for long periods of time. When Evan was four, his mother died of leukemia. Morgan left the navy and took a job as the captain of a cruise ship. Since he couldn't have his son with him, he sent Evan to live with my husband Roger and me."

"So, in a sense, Evan lost both his mother and father at a young age."

"Yes. What a despondent little boy he was for a few years! He spent most of his time alone: reading, doing puzzles, playing video games, watching T.V. Roger gradually got him interested in team sports: soccer, baseball, and later basketball; eventually Evan became an excellent team player and developed friends on the team."

"What was Evan like in high school?" Ruth asked. As a freshman, Ruth had found him conceited and narcissistic, but Gloria undoubtedly had not seen those traits in her grandson.

"He was a typical teenager, mainly interested in himself. During the summertime, he spent time with his father on the cruise ship, and when Evan returned home, we had a little difficulty in handling him for a while. I think that Morgan was too permissive aboard ship, and when Evan came home, he rebelled about the restrictions Roger set. Good behavior and obedience were required in our household."

"I was just acquainted with him in high school, but we both went to Berkeley for college, where I got to know him a little better."

"His first year there, Roger had a heart attack and died, and Evan was left without parental guidance. I was coping with grief, and Morgan was still sailing around in his own aquatic world. So, the 'A' student became a 'D' student. Morgan continued to pay tuition and college expenses, but three years later, he had had enough; he gave Evan the ultimatum to 'shape up or ship out.'"

"Thanks, Gloria, for sharing that with me. It helps me to better understand Evan."

"You're welcome, Ruth. Evan needs someone like you in his life," Gloria concluded.

Ruth went out to the garden with a glass of iced tea and seated herself on the wicker settee, from which she could watch the two different activities going on. On the lawn to the right, Ralph and Oscar were playing croquet in a hotly contested manner. There was a loud crack of Ralph's mallet on the ball. "I'll get you for that," shouted Oscar, as he responded by sending Ralph's ball out of bounds. Ralph shouted back, "You fiend!"

"Hey, you two," yelled Judy, who was seated on the bench around the roses. "You'll break the ball and my eardrums!"

On the lawn to the left, Dr. Sandler and Peter were playing a very civilized game of badminton. Since there were no markings on the grass to determine the boundaries of the court, they had agreed upon their own demarcations. They were playing according to the badminton rules they had agreed to follow: the server must hit the shuttlecock from below the waist and propel it over the net in one motion; the opponent must return it in one motion; neither player is allowed to bounce the birdie or hit it into the net. Both Peter and Dr. Sandler were playing enthusiastically but jovially. Ruth noticed that Peter was tempering his speed and endurance to Dr. Sandler's age. Peter won the set two to one, but Dr. Sandler was happy with the outcome.

When Dr. Sandler left the garden, Peter came to sit next to Ruth.

"You looked like an athlete out there, Peter," Ruth complimented him.

"Dr. Sandler is quite fit for his age and is still a good opponent," he answered.

"I thought that you handled the difference in your ages with sensitivity," she continued.

"As counselors, we're trained to do that, aren't we?"

Ruth smiled at him. "You're a very humble counselor, Peter Paulson."

Chapter XIV: The Story of Creation

Ruth and Peter entered the library at the same time on Monday. After Peter seated himself, Ruth chose a seat opposite in the circle so that she had a good vision of him. The group began filing in, the men taking seats next to Peter and the women adjacent to Ruth.

Peter announced the topic for discussion: God's creation of the world. "Today," he said, "we will be reading Chapters 1 and 2 of the 'Book of Genesis.' I see that you have all brought your Bibles, and that there is a variety of versions here. I will be using the *King James Study Bible* because of its explanatory notes and references and because I personally love the poetic language of the text. Please follow along in your own Bible as I read from mine. I will pause at the end of a portion of verses so that you can reread the verses silently in your version, and then we will discuss those verses.

"Let's start with two questions: Who wrote 'Genesis' and when was it written? Most Biblical scholars attribute the authorship to Moses, who lived from 1525 B.C. to 1405 B.C. Moses was raised as the adopted son of the Pharaoh of Egypt and, therefore, was well-educated in the Egyptian language. From his native heritage, he was familiar with the spoken Hebrew language. The oral story of the creation was not put into written form until 850 B.C. by an unnamed author who called God 'Jehovah.'

"The word *genesis* means *the beginning*. The style of the writer is poetic, whereas some books of the Bible are written in historical style, such as the gospels of the *New Testament*; or chronological, such as the *Book of Numbers*; or prophetical, such as the *Book of Isaiah*.

"Let's begin with Verses 1 and 2 of Chapter 1: 'In the beginning God created the heaven and the earth. And the earth was without form and void; and the darkness was upon the face of the deep. And the Spirit of God moved upon the face of the waters.'"

"Paraphrase verses 1 and 2, using your own words. Don't wait to be called on," said Peter.

Elizabeth said, "The beginning sentences are the preface to the rest of the story."

Judy said, "Putting it in my own words, God created both heaven and earth from nothing."

Dr. Sandler – "The Bible describes earth as being without form and void. To me, that means that matter existed, but it had not been put into the shape of planets, suns, etc. in the universe."

Oscar – "God had not yet created light; so, there was no distinction between light and darkness."

Peter – "What is meant by the 'Spirit of God'?"

Elizabeth – "God's divine nature, His spiritual nature."

Gloria – "It could also mean the Holy Spirit. Since God is a Triune God, that part of the Godhead would be present."

Peter - "The Spirit of God moved – what is meant by 'moved'?"

Cindy – "God started the process of creating. But I don't understand what is meant by the 'face of the waters.'"

Peter – "That will be explained in verses 6 through 8."

Peter continued by reading verses 3, 4, and 5 as the group followed in their Bibles - 'And God said: let there be light, and there was light. And God saw the light that it was good; and God divided the light from the darkness. And God called the light Day and the darkness he called Night. And the evening and the morning were the first day.'"

Ralph – "God created the sun and the moon on the first day and divided time into morning and evening."

Peter – "No, the sun and moon in **our** solar system are not created until verse 16."

Dr. Sandler – "I think that God created light by the stars (the suns) at different periods of time, the older ones being the earliest created and, the newer suns as the universe expanded. The sun and moon within **our** solar system were not the first to be created."

Judy – "How do you explain the 'morning and the evening were the first day'?"

Dr. Sandler – "The earth at this point had not been created; so, 'morning' and 'evening' could refer to epochs of time, not twenty-four hours."

Elizabeth – "Remember. 'Genesis' is not a historical book; it is poetic, symbolic, open to shades of meaning. Furthermore, it evolved from an oral story, which had many different narrators throughout the millennium."

Moving on, Peter said, "I'm going to paraphrase verses 6 through 10 – 'God separated the waters under and above the firmament and then gathered the waters together to form land.' How do you interpret the 'firmament' and the 'waters?'"

Dr. Sandler – "The seas were not distinguishable from the vapor over the earth. The firmament is the atmosphere surrounding the earth, which we sometimes call sky. In order for life to begin on earth, the land needed to be separated from the seas, and a protective shield of atmosphere had to be formed around the earth to protect life from the sun's rays."

Elizabeth – "The basic elements for life are earth, air and water. Each needed to be created and put into a form that would foster and sustain life."

Peter continued. "Verses 10 through 13 are about God's creation of botanical life on land (the soil.) He created trees, plants, and grasses, 'each according to its own kind. The seed was within, according to its own kind.'"

Peter – "What is the meaning of 'according to **its own kind'**?"

Cindy – "He created different types of trees and grasses, etc.'"

Peter – "What is the meaning of 'the seed was **in itself**, according to its own kind'?"

Ralph – "An apple tree can produce apples which have seeds that will grow into other apple trees if they are planted, but an apple seed cannot become a redwood tree."

Peter – "Good example, Ralph. Considering the phrase, 'according to its own kind,' this has become part of the debate about Darwin's theory of evolution versus creationism. Darwin purported that all life evolved from a single-cell organism, which contradicts the story of the creation told in the Bible."

Peter continued by paraphrasing the text for Day 4: "God created the sun to rule by day and the moon to rule by night.' Since other solar systems have suns and moons, I interpret this to mean **our** sun and **ou**r moon. In Verse 15, the writer states that the sun and the moon are for light on the **earth** and for **signs**, **seasons**, **days**, and **year**s. I interpret this as the establishment of **our time period** upon earth."

Judy – "How do **signs** relate to time?"

Dr. Sandler – "An example might be the planet, Venus, appearing in the sky as a sign at a given period of time."

Peter – "Why did God establish seasons, days, and years?"

No one responded. Ruth joined the discussion – "All grasses, plants, and trees need a cycle of life, a time to sprout, grow, mature, produce fruit and seed, die, and start all over again with a new seed sprouting. God created this cycle for the regularity of nature so that plants could flourish. Plants need daylight for growing and reproducing and nighttime for resting and regaining vitality. The seasons of spring, summer, and fall allow crops to be planted, to grow and produce, and to be harvested. Then winter allows time for the soil to lie dormant, enabling it to replenish itself."

Peter – "Thank you, Ruth. I can see that your mother had a gardener's green thumb." Ruth nodded. Peter continued paraphrasing. "'On the fifth and sixth days, God created, again according to its own kind, all of the fish in the sea, all of the fowls of the air, and all of the land creatures and animals. In each case, He ordered His created ones to become fruitful and multiply, and replenish the earth. His last creation was man, whom He created in His own image.'"

Oscar – "What is meant by 'in His own image'?"

Cindy – "God couldn't have meant 'physical appearance' because God is a spiritual being."

Dr. Sandler – "God made man with a body, mind, and soul - a creature superior to others. Before man, God created some creatures with only rudimentary bodies, some with more developed bodies and instinctual minds, some with minds capable only of limited reasoning. But only to man did he give a body, a mind capable of complicated reasoning, and a soul."

Elizabeth – "Only to mankind did God give the ability to distinguish between good and evil, and the free will to either seek a relationship with him or to live selfishly. So; God made man special."

Peter – "At the end of each phase of creation, God remarked that 'It was good.' Out of God's creative mind came only goodness, and we come back to the age-old question: How did evil enter the story?"

Judy - "Evil, in the form of the devil, was present but not recognized."

Elizabeth – "I agree with Judy. The **ability for evil** was there. However, evil did not become known by Adam and Eve until they disobeyed God's order. God had created them with free will, and they chose to defy God; thus, evil manifested itself."

Ralph – "For me, the existence of evil has always been a stumbling block to having faith."

Peter – "Faith requires a leap from the material world into the spiritual. It is more difficult to believe than it is to see."

Dr. Sandler – "Reverend Keller, the author of *The Reason for God,* wrote that doubts can trouble each of us. Like a human body needs an antibody to fight an infection, we need faith to conquer our doubts. No view of God can be **materially** proven, but faith gives us the antibody."

Peter – "I recently read about Francis Collins, a research scientist who was head of the Genome Project. As he learned more and more through his research, he began to doubt that nature could have created itself, and he eventually turned from a belief in atheism to Christianity. He felt that only a supernatural, self-created being could have been the primary mover. He pointed to the orderliness of the universe, which could not just have happened by chance: the constants of physics, such as the speed of light, and the gravitational forces of celestial bodies. Add to that, the regularity of nature, the intricacies of the human body, the uniqueness of individual items, plus the existence of beauty. All of these point to a creator with a master mind."

"Thank you, Peter, for that antidote to doubt," said Dr. Sandler.

Peter nodded and smiled. "Ruth," he said, "do you have a closing comment to our discussion?"

Ruth – "Just a personal one. When I have found myself feeling awed by looking up at countless stars in the night sky, or have experienced the beauty of a gorgeous garden, or have felt enraptured by listening to a choir of two hundred voices, I want to thank God, the Creator, for these gifts, and not the god of chance." Everyone nodded.

As the group began leaving, Peter touched Ruth's shoulder. "Meet me in the chapel in fifteen minutes?" he asked.

"See you there, Peter."

Chapter XV: Becoming Friends

Peter looked refreshed as he arrived at the chapel. He was carrying two lemonades and gave one to Ruth. Sitting next to her, he brought out two photographs from his shirt pocket and handed them to her.

"I took these photos when I was on a hiking trip with my friend at the U of A. The first one was taken at sunset when we were halfway up Mt. Lemmon."

"What brilliant shades of orange flaming across the sky!" remarked Ruth.

"The sunsets in Tucson are spectacular. It's the desert dust in the air that causes the brilliance. The second one was taken when we were at the top of the mountain, and night had fallen. The city lights were far below, so they could not obstruct the view of the night sky. There were no clouds, and when we looked up, we saw what seemed like a trillion stars. We both knew that each star was a sun within its own solar system, and we both were awed with a glimpse of the vastness of the universe." He paused, waiting for Ruth to lift her eyes to him. "When you said today at the close of our session how you had been awed and enraptured by God's gifts, I suddenly realized that you and I are kindred spirits. I'm glad you came here, Ruth."

"I'm glad, too."

***

Following dinner, when Ruth was having coffee in the lounge, Evan approached her. "Want to watch a DVD with me this evening?" he asked.

"What is it?" she inquired.

"*The Bishop's Wife.* It's an old black-and-white starring Cary Grant, David Niven, and Loretta Young."

"I haven't seen that one," Ruth responded, "but that's a good cast."

"O.K. My apartment or yours?"

"Mine," she answered. "You can bring the popcorn and the movie."

Evan arrived at Ruth's door an hour later with two bowls of popcorn, a six-pack of beer, and the DVD. They seated themselves in the two leather chairs and shared the ottoman throughout the movie. Evan's cell phone rang twice during the movie. He went out into the hall to answer it and spoke for a while each time.

When the movie was over, Ruth said, "You missed a lot of the story."

"I've seen it before, Ruth. I wanted you to see it because the three movie characters relate to each other like the three of us do: Peter, you and me."

"How so?"

"Peter is the bishop, who is faced with the problem of finding donations to build a cathedral. I am the angel, who is sent to help him solve his problem." Ruth snickered. "I fall in love with the bishop's wife. That's you. The wife is torn between her duty to the bishop and her attraction to the angel."

"The only similarity that I see is that the bishop and Peter are both spiritual leaders," commented Ruth.

"No. **Preachy Peter** is like the bishop, who forgets that his wife needs to be treated like a woman, whereas the angel is attracted to her and finds himself falling in love with her."

"Peter and I don't have a romantic relationship, but neither do you and I, Evan."

"We can change that, Ruth."

"For now, I'm happy being a friend to both Peter and you. And Evan, please don't portray Peter in a derogatory manner. It doesn't enhance my opinion of you."

Evan had no response to Ruth's criticism, but his actions spoke clearly. He lifted up his can of beer, said "Bottoms up," and chugged down the beer. Rising from the chair, he said, "Keep the rest of the six-pack, Ruth." She followed him to the door and handed him the DVD and the two empty bowls.

"Goodnight, Evan. Thanks for the movie and the refreshment."

He gave her a quick kiss on the cheek and left.

***

Ruth left the following day for Los Gatos for a weekend visit. Her parents were just unloading their suitcases from the Lincoln sedan when she pulled into the driveway.

"Where have you been?" Ruth asked.

"I had business in Seattle," answered her father. "We drove this time so that we could follow Highway 1 up the coast through California, Oregon, and Washington."

"It was spectacular!" her mother exclaimed. "The ocean kept changing from gray-blue to green-blue and then to yellow-blue when the sun was peeking from behind a cloud."

"At times the ocean was turbulent when the tide was coming in," her father added. "We kept stopping at pullouts so that we could enjoy the crashing of the waves against the rocks." He paused. "But, how are you, Ruthie?"

"Good. Working hard, learning, getting to know the residents."

"That's my girl!" he responded.

Mr. Martin carried the bags into the entrance hall and headed for his study to check on his email messages. Mrs. Martin gave Ruth a hug and said, "I'll get us a snack from the kitchen while you take your things up to your room. Take time to settle in; when you come back down, we'll have a visit." When Ruth returned, her mother had lemonade and gingersnap cookies waiting in the lounge. Posie was asleep on her lap.

"How did your circle meeting go?" her mother asked.

"Let me steal Posie from your lap while I tell you about it." Now awake, Posie gladly exchanged one lap for another. "The meeting went well. Everyone participated, and I learned a lot about them from their speaking and interaction with each other. Since you are a counselor to me, Mom, I can share the details with you."

"Of course you can. I will never meet any of the residents."

"Well, as they entered the library where the meeting was held, the men seated themselves next to Peter and to each other, and the women next to each other, with Judy next to Peter and Gloria next to me. Gloria has taken a special liking to me; she's Evan's grandmother, you know."

Mrs. Martin nodded. "What did you learn from their seating of themselves?" she asked.

"Who was comfortable with whom."

"Good observation, Ruth. You're beginning to sound like a counselor. So, what was your original impression of them?"

"Gloria seems open-minded and accepting of all of the others. Judy is observant and inquisitive and looks to Peter for guidance. Dr. Sandler is very knowledgeable in science as well as other subjects, but he is not a disbeliever. Elizabeth is an ex-college professor in literature. She is the best-read one in the group. Being a maiden lady, she has spent a lot of time either seeking or imparting knowledge."

"Hmm," responded Mrs. Martin, lifting her eyebrows.

"She annoys some of the others. They feel like she is lecturing them. Cindy, especially, who spent her life as a housewife, feels like Elizabeth belittles her.

"I can picture that," responded her mother. "Nobody likes a know-it-all."

"Oscar, who is a buffoon, enjoys frustrating Elizabeth. He and his friend Ralph play off each other by exchanging barbs, which can disrupt the flow of the discussion."

"Just bad boys enjoying being with other bad boys," commented her mother.

"Actually, they do add humor to the discussion, and most of the group aren't bothered by them. Two somewhat juvenile grown men," she added. "That about sums it up for now, Mom."

"You haven't mentioned Peter, the head of the circle."

"I need time to know Peter. I can tell from his handling of the group that he has a sense of humor and is sensitive, kind, and knowledgeable."

"He sounds like a 'good-un', Ruthie."

"Time will tell, Mom. Can we visit more later? I'd like to play piano for a while."

"Please do. I'll listen."

Ruth looked through her stack of music and selected a Debussy arabesque and a Satie waltz. When she finished, she said, "They're so beautiful, Mom. They always inspire me."

"Me, too," her mother responded. The Debussy piece makes me think of a brook bubbling along, and Satie's waltz is not like a typical waltz by Strauss, but more of a romantic suggestion of a waltz, like remembering a dream."

"Yes," agreed Ruth. "Now for a change to the world of Handel." She played "Arioso" in *largo* tempo then contrasted it with

"Allegretto," which contained staccato notes that enlivened the melody."

"Dad and I certainly got our money's worth with all of those piano lessons you had, Ruthie. I hope that you are keeping up your skills at the center."

"There is a beautiful Steinway grand in the lounge, but there are often residents in the room, and I don't want to disturb them."

'Nuts! They can go to their rooms if they want solitude. In the latest AARP magazine, there was an article about memory and music. Neuroscience now has proof of music's positive effects on the minds of the elderly, in fact, on all of our minds. So, disturb the residents! You'll be doing them a favor."

**

In the lounge, following dinner, Mr. and Mrs. Martin seated themselves on a couch in front of the fireplace; Ruth took the couch that was opposite. Posie trailed into the room and rubbed herself against Mrs. Martin's legs on her way to Ruth's lap.

"Mom informs me that you are getting to know a nice young man at the center, Ruth," said her father.

"Only through our jobs. We work together in counseling and spiritual guidance. I don't think that he is particularly attracted to me. I never catch him looking me over or just watching me."

"Ha! Some of us men can be quite subtle. I found ways to admire your mother without her noticing." Mrs. Martin smiled.

"Your father and I started out by just enjoying each other's company."

"Peter and I are in each other's company most of the day, but the closest he's come to attraction is the other day when he called me a *kindred spirit*."

Her parents looked at each other, and then Mr. Martin walked over to the large Webster Dictionary resting on a stand and said, "Let's see what Mr. Webster has to say about the word *kindred.* Here it is: it is listed in adjective, verb, and noun forms. The verb *kindle* means *to start a fire*. The adjective *kindred* mean *congenial*. The noun *kindred* mean *a relationship by blood or marriage.* The word *kindling* means *something used to start a fire*."

"Remember when we used to go camping, Ruthie. Dad and I would ask you to gather up clumps of dried grass and twigs to put under a log. Then Dad would put a match to the kindling to start the fire going. When the log was alight, it would keep us warm all night."

"For your mother and me, the fire is still alight," he said, squeezing his wife's hand. Turning to Ruth, he added, "Being called a *kindred spirit* is promising, Ruthie."

The doorbell sounded. Mrs. Martin asked Ruth if she was expecting anybody.

"No one," Ruth answered. "I'll go to the door." *Perhaps it's someone for Dad*, she thought as she walked into the hall. She opened the door to find Evan standing there.

Chapter XVI: Peter's Absence

"Surprise, Ruth! I just came by on the chance that you were here."

"I am surprised. I came home to be with my parents."

"Yes, I figured. Since you're in town, would you like to go to an after-theater party with me? I'd like you to meet some of my theater friends."

"I didn't know you had any theater friends. Besides, I'm having a lovely evening with my parents. We're just about ready to watch a DVD. You're welcome to join us."

"O.K. The party won't get going until midnight."

Ruth took him into the lounge, explained his sudden appearance to her parents, and offered him coffee. "Are you interested in movies?" Mr. Martin asked.

"Yes, but not so much the movie itself as the making of the movie and the trailer to promote it. Friends of mine in San Jose have a start-up trailer making business, which I have invested in."

"You certainly have a variety of interests," commented Mr. Martin.

Mrs. Martin informed Evan that they were about to watch a movie version of the stage play, *Kismet*. "The main characters in the story are both actors and singers because it is primarily a musical. Do you like musicals? They're not everyone's cup of tea." Evan responded that he had not seen a musical for a long time. "You may be too young to be familiar with the cast," she continued. "Howard Keel, Anne Blythe, and Vic Damone had beautiful, trained voices and were popular during their time."

"I've seen Anne Blythe in an older movie with Joan Crawford. She was a good actress. I didn't know that she could sing, too."

Ruth led the way to the family room, which was equipped with surround-sound speakers, a large screen, projection equipment, and several comfortable sofas for seating. Mr. and Mrs. Martin took one of the sofas, and Ruth and Evan seated themselves on another. Posie, who had trailed along, jumped up and settled herself on Ruth's lap and next to Evan, hoping for attention from both. Mr. Martin offered Evan a choice of wine, and Mrs. Martin brought snacks from the adjoining kitchen.

Throughout the movie, Evan appeared restless. He crossed and uncrossed his legs, shifted around on the sofa, and paid more attention to Posie than to the film. At the end of the movie, Mrs. Martin remarked that the arias were based on Russian folk music written by the composer, Borodin. She added, "When Anne Blythe and Vic Damone sang their beautiful duet, I was transported into the garden they were in, with the aroma of roses and jasmine, among tropical foliage and peacocks."

"You're a romantic, my dear," said her husband, "and I love that about you." Turning to Evan, he asked if he had enjoyed the movie.

"Yes," he said, "but my favorite movies are action movies." None of the Martins responded to his comment.

"What now, Ruth?" asked her mother. "This is bedtime for Dad and me."

"I'd like to demonstrate our surround system to Evan before he leaves."

"Absolutely." Ruth's parents said 'goodnight' and left the room to go upstairs. Ruth demonstrated various attributes of the equipment and then said, "Let me play a CD which captures the richness of the sound. What is your favorite type of music, Evan?"

"Music with a good beat, something to get the juices going, with drums and guitars, and repetition."

"We don't have any CDs to fit that description unless we turn on the radio, but that wouldn't demonstrate the sound that the equipment is capable of."

"O.K. You choose a CD."

From the collection of CDs, Ruth selected a recording of Smetana's symphonic poem entitled *The Moldau*. She gave a brief introduction to it to help Evan to listen and appreciate the music: "*The Moldau,* she explained, was written in the late 19th century by Smetana, a Czeck composer. It is called a symphonic poem because it is written for a symphonic orchestra, and it paints a picture of the flow of the River Moldau through the Czechoslovakian countryside on its way to the city of Prague. Smetana uses all of the basic elements of music to describe the river's journey: the tempo of the music ranges from slow to fast to depict the flow of the water; various instruments are used to paint the scenery: at first, the woodwinds depict the bubbling of a brook that starts in the Bohemian Forest; then brass and rhythmic instruments are used to depict village life along the way. As the river approaches Prague, it becomes fast and strong. You will hear this as the harmony in the music becomes heavier with chords and the volume of the music increases."

Ruth started the CD and Evan listened as he held Posie. Towards the end of the recording, when the turmoil of the river began, Posie jumped down and scampered into the kitchen for the comfort of her dog food. When the music ended, Evan said, "I'm impressed with the equipment, but I prefer my type of music to yours, Ruth."

Ruth countered his statement: "A composer who uses most if not all of the elements of music, such as tempo, melody, harmony, volume, and a variety of instrumentation, creates music that is rich in flavor. It's like sitting down to enjoy a five-course dinner. Both my type of music and yours will keep the listener from starving, but do you want to go through life on just bread and milk?"

"Not everyone has **your** love of music, Ruth, and that's good. The world needs people who are willing to just put the bread and the milk on the table."

"You're right, Evan. I didn't mean to put you down."

"It's time for me to go. After the party, I'm staying with my friend tonight." He followed Ruth to the front door, embraced her, and said, "See you back at the center."

***

When Ruth returned to the center the following day, she found that Peter was gone. She went to the office to ask Edith about it. "Peter had to leave for a family emergency in Tucson," she said, and handed Ruth a note that he had left. In his note, Peter explained that his father had suddenly collapsed. He wasn't sure how long he would be gone. Meanwhile, would she handle his appointments until he returns. If she finds that she does not have enough time to prepare for the circle meeting, the session could be postponed. He ended the note: "Please pray for me and my family. God bless. Peter." Ruth went immediately to the chapel, where she prayed for Peter and his family and then for herself. When she finished meditating, she returned to Edith's office for a list of Peter's appointments. In her apartment, Ruth compiled a new list of appointments which she would handle in the coming days.

Her first appointment the following day was with Gloria. "I'm so glad," Gloria began, "that Evan is dating you, Ruth, rather than the typical girls he chooses."

"We're just friends, Gloria."

"I've seen the way he looks at you. Anyway, I want to tell you about his father, Morgan, to help you to understand Evan better."

"O.K. Do you mind if I take a few notes?"

"No. Please go ahead." Gloria continued. "Morgan was the child of my husband, Roger and me. When Morgan was a little boy, he loved the water. Roger taught him to swim at age three, and Morgan loved playing in the pool. We bought him different types of toy boats: sailing and fishing boats, rafts, cargo boats, military boats, and Morgan created his own make-believe world on the ocean.

"When Morgan was high school age, he wanted to go to a military school, but Roger and I wanted him with us at home, so we encouraged him to study hard and apply to the naval academy at Annapolis for college. In his sophomore year, he met Evangeline, who was attending a college nearby. Morgan fell madly in love with her; she was stunningly beautiful (Evan has inherited her features), and sweet-natured.

"Morgan and Evangeline did not want to wait until they graduated before they married, so Roger and I helped them with rent for an apartment and other living expenses. By the end of their junior year, Evan was born. After graduation, Morgan stayed at Annapolis for a master's degree, and Evangeline enjoyed being a wife and mother. What a happy threesome they were! I'm so glad that Roger and I helped them financially so that they could have those joyful years together.

"When Morgan finished college and was commissioned, their lives changed. Morgan was on ship duty for long periods of time, and Evangeline was alone with baby Evan." Gloria paused. "I think that Evangeline's loneliness and depression led to her cancer and death when Evan was four. Morgan resigned from the navy and became a captain of a cruise ship, and he sent Evan to live with Roger and me.

"You know, Ruth, I think that Roger and I did the best we could in raising Evan, but our best wasn't good enough. Evan was caught between following in the footsteps of a neglectful father and a grandfather trying to be a father. As for me, I knew that I could not fulfill the role of a mother in addition to being a grandmother. To Evan, I became just 'Gloria.' Ruth, I wish that he would at least treat me like a grandmother."

"He's a very busy young man, with his work and his charities."

"And he's also the POA and trustee of my estate. I could take that workload off him and turn it over to my lawyer. What do you think, Ruth?"

"Why not talk it over with Evan and perhaps hint that you would like to see more of him." Gloria agreed, thanked Ruth, and left, saying "Let's have lunch together soon."

Ruth made some notes about the appointment, answered a phone call, and then left her study to walk down to the dock. Evan was just returning from the dock. "Hi, Ruth. How did it go with Gloria?" he asked.

"You know I can't talk to you about that."

"O.K., Madam Counselor!" He tipped his hat and continued by her.

Chapter XVII: Substituting for Peter

Ruth substituted for Peter at her next appointment. Ralph came into her study with an armful of picture albums, which he set on the coffee table.

"I'm taking Peter's place today," began Ruth. "How can I help you?"

"I need some guidance about my relationship with my son, Brooks. Do you know him?"

"Just briefly. Evan introduced him to me."

"My relationship with Brooks has not been good for some time."

"Relationships between father and son can be complicated, often stemming back to the previous generation. What was your own father like, Ralph?"

"He was a very successful man, self-made. As a young man, he worked in a factory that manufactured shipping containers. He gradually raised himself up to become the manager and eventually bought the factory. Then he expanded the local company into an international one. That meant a lot of traveling, domestic and abroad. He was gone from home a lot, but occasionally he took my mother and me with him on a trip. I got to know parts of Canada, England, France, Italy, Portugal, Korea, and Japan. My mother was an amateur photographer, and she kept albums of our travels." He pointed to the albums on the table.

"Did you and your mother have a good relationship?"

"Very good. She was the one who took an interest in my school, my friends, and my future. When I left home to go to college, she divorced my father. She had had enough of his self-centeredness. The divorce didn't seem to bother him; he just continued devoting himself to making money." He paused. "Until he died."

"You inherited your father's business?"

"Yes, but I eventually sold it and invested in real estate, which is now Brooks' game."

"Why do you say 'game'?"

"I don't think he works very hard at it and, like a card player, he keeps his hand hidden."

"Has he always been secretive?"

"Yes, but more so since Lily, my wife, died. That was ten years ago."

"How did her death affect each of you?"

"Shortly after Lily died, I met Reverend Howard. I was very depressed, and he encouraged me to 'seek God instead of Mammon,' as he put it. The reverend suggested a move to the center, and here I am, warts and all."

"How has that affected your relationship with Brooks?"

"I've become less materialistic, and Brooks has gone the other way. He finds me foolish and often pokes fun at my new-found beliefs."

"Are you worried about his spiritual welfare?"

"Yes. I don't want to see him going the wrong way in life, but I did not set a good example when he was growing up. I have not been a good role model."

"Ralph, no human can convince another to change his heart. That is the working of the Holy Spirit. The Holy Spirit will continue to 'knock on Brooks' door,' but only Brooks can let the Spirit in."

"Then there's nothing I can do now."

"Yes, there is, Ralph. Lead by the example of your present life. Then pray and keep praying."

"I'm still a beginner at praying."

"No prayer or thought is too small. Try the chapel. It's a great place to still your mind and let your soul speak."

"Thanks, Ruth." As he arose to go, he motioned to the travel albums and asked, "Do you care to look at Lily's photography?"

"Of course. Please leave the albums with me."

***

The next morning, Ruth took her breakfast out to the patio and sat at a table near the lawn, where sparrows were hopping about. Oscar, dressed in jeans, a T-shirt, tennis shoes, and a baseball cap, had set up a putting green; Ruth watched him until she had finished eating. On her way upstairs, she met Evan coming down the stairs.

"Ah! The fresh flower of the morn!" he greeted her.

"Good morning," she answered. "It's a lovely day."

"What do you hear from Peter?" Evan asked.

"Nothing, but no news is good news, I hope."

"He's too busy having fun, I guess."

"Hardly. His father is very ill, Evan."

"I know that, Ruth. I was just joking. You needn't be so **touchy**."

"Have a good day, Evan." *I could have done without that conversation*, she thought to herself. She knew that Oscar would be difficult to deal with; consequently, she had prepared herself with food and coffee and the fresh air and sparrows in the garden, and she did not appreciate Evan's insensitivity. She went to the bathroom, brushed her teeth and doused cold water on her face; then she seated herself at her desk and reread Peter's notes about Oscar.

When Oscar entered, he was still wearing his baseball cap, now on backwards. He seated himself in one of the leather chairs and stretched his legs out on the ottoman; Ruth remained seated at her desk. Holding his folder in her hand, she said, "I see, Oscar, that the last time you met with Peter, you discussed your family background."

"Yes. The Olivers are well-known," he said proudly.

"How so?"

"In the areas of money and sports. My grandfather had five sons; the oldest was my father, Alan Oliver, who was a professional golfer. You've heard of him. Right?" Ruth shook her head 'no'. Oscar tried again to impress her. "You've heard of the Oliver fortune?" Ruth shook her head 'no' again. "Well, my father set out to become the wealthiest of the boys in his family, and he succeeded. When he died, his four brothers were very impressed with his fortune."

"What happened to the fortune?" asked Ruth. "Was he able to take it with him when he died?"

"Of course not. He left it to me, and I haven't been selfish with it. I've been generous with the center here and with some of Evan's charities and with my own family."

"Tell me about your family."

"My wife, Trudy, and I are divorced. We had two daughters and a son named Jake. They're all constantly in need of money; both daughters married worthless husbands, and Jake runs an unsuccessful shelter for dogs and cats with his partner, Evan."

"How did you happen to come here?" asked Ruth.

"Ralph and I were members of the same country club; that is, I am the owner of the golf course, and Ralph played there."

"That's an important distinction," commented Ruth, with a smile on her face.

"I realize that you think I'm a braggart, Ruth, but I can't brag about my son, and I can't manage the money issue with him."

"What do you mean by that?"

"When he comes around asking for money, I call him Jakey. His middle name is Edward, so I call him Jakey – Jake E. Get it?"

"I'm afraid I don't."

"Well, Jakey is a child's name, and when he starts sniveling and sulking like a four-year-old, I treat him like a child."

"Is he afraid of you, Oscar?"

"He shouldn't be. I've never mistreated him. When he was a child, he preferred to play with his sisters, and I didn't force him to play with boys. In high school, when he didn't want to sign up for football, basketball, soccer, or even baseball, I didn't make him."

"What were his interests in high school?"

"Chess, book club, drama."

"It sounds like he was interested more in activities involving the mind."

"Yes, and they didn't help him to become a successful adult; instead, he became a successful **bum**."

"In your eyes, Oscar, but not in God's. If God didn't love each of us, there would be no spiritual help for any of us. Oscar, you admitted that you are incapable of handling the 'money issue' with Jake. However, you are asking help from your point of view, which is a limited one. You have only a glimpse into Jake's thinking and feelings. I think that you need to discuss this further with Peter when he returns."

"I agree. Peter will understand."

Chapter XVIII: Peter's Return

Ruth checked with Edith a few days later to find out if she had heard from Peter. She informed Ruth that Peter would be returning on Saturday evening, and that Reverend Howard would be meeting him at the Sacramento Airport. She added: "After Peter rests up, he would like to meet with you following the video service tomorrow."

The service was just getting started when Peter walked into the lounge. All of the residents waved a silent greeting to him. Smiling at Ruth, he seated himself next to her. Out of the corner of her eye, Ruth looked him over. His skin had a glow to it, as though he had spent time in the sun, and he had gotten a haircut. *He's good looking, in a next-door neighbor way*, she thought.

"Welcome back, Peter," she said when the service ended.

"Thank you, Ruth. Let's get our lunch and take it into the garden, where we can visit."

Peter first asked Ruth about herself and then about the appointments she had taken for him.

"I felt that my meeting with Ralph went well. I left you notes about it in your folder. My meeting with Oscar was unproductive; so, I suggested that he take his 'issue' to you when you returned. Sorry."

"Don't worry, Ruth. Oscar would be difficult for any counselor to handle."

"It's hard for me to find a redeeming quality in Oscar. I know that's very judgmental of me."

"Trying to help your fellow man is very difficult if he feels that you are judging him. People have different ways of reacting to criticism. No doubt you have heard a person say, 'Look who's calling the kettle black.'"

"Yes," Ruth agreed, or 'Stop criticizing me. It's my life!'"

"Or 'I'll handle my own affairs, and God can judge me in the end.'"

"Or 'Don't blame me. I am not responsible for what the other guy does.'"

Ruth said, "That last example describes Oliver. He is incapable of seeing that he has mistreated his son Jake. Poor Jake!"

"Yes. They both need help. I'm sure we'll be discussing them for some time, Ruth." Changing the subject, Peter said, "I'm sorry I had to leave you with extra duties, but my family needed me immediately."

"Did your father have a heart attack? We weren't told any of the details."

"He did have a heart attack, but it was brought on by a hit-and-run car accident. A motorist plowed through a red light at high speed and hit my dad's car broadside. Another motorist saw the accident and called 911. Dad was unconscious; his head had been struck on the metal of the door when his car spun out of control. When he remained unconscious, Mom called my brother, Robert, and me to come home. Meanwhile, the doctor ordered a brain scan, which showed activity in Dad's brain, but the doctor could give us no assurance as to how long the coma would last or even if Dad would recover."

"That must have been a very tense time for your family," said Ruth.

"Yes. Dad was hooked up to a breathing machine, and we all stood around, watching him. Mom kept saying, 'Talk to him, boys; he can hear you.' She wouldn't leave his bedside. My brothers and I caught a few naps between being at the hospital and keeping things going at home. Two days later, Dad regained consciousness, looked around at all of us, and said, 'I'm hungry.' We all were hungry; so, we ordered hospital food for breakfast."

"That's a beautiful description of how your family reacted in a crucial situation. On a lighter note, how did you get your Tucson tan?"

"I sat with Dad in the garden as he recuperated. We had some very good father and son talks about the past and the future. I told him about our working together, Ruth, and showed him a picture of you."

"I didn't know that you have a picture of me."

"Yes. I took it here in the garden when you weren't looking." Ruth smiled and changed the subject.

"What about the motorist who hit your father?"

"The police came to our house several times with information about him. He was a young illegal immigrant from El Salvador. He had no proper identification, no insurance, and no car. He had stolen the one he was in when he hit my dad."

"You said that he was a hit-and-run driver."

"Yes, also what the police call a **got-away**."

"**Got-away** from whom?"

"From the Border Patrol. Most illegals enter the U.S. and turn themselves over to the Border Patrol to wait for the immigration authorities to grant them asylum. **Got-aways**, who evade the patrol, are often brought in by smugglers, such as the Sinaloa Cartel, a dangerous criminal group."

"It sounds like Tucson is becoming a dangerous place to live," commented Ruth.

"Yes. Migrants are coming in faster than the Border Patrol can process them; so lately, the patrol are releasing busloads of migrants into the streets of Tucson every half-hour. The city can't handle the surge in population: there is an emergency overload in hospitals, insufficient law enforcement, inability of the court to keep up with their case overload, and overcrowding and language problems in schools."

"Are you worried about your parents living in Tucson?"

"Yes, and my brother Colin, as well. He is a history professor at the University of Arizona. While Robert and I were there, we had a family discussion about the migrant problem."

"It's not just a local problem, is it?"

"No. Millions of people from all over the world are coming here. Colin, the history professor, pointed out that huge migrations of people have taken place since the Bronze Age, including migrations during the reign of the Roman emperors, the partition of India into Pakistan and India, the Diaspora in Italy, the European immigration to the U.S. from 1880 to 1915, and the displacement of people today in various parts of the globe. Robert pointed out that our own citizens are moving from one state to another – New York to Florida, California to Texas, etc."

Ruth said, "The number of people moving from one place to another for various reasons creates an unstable environment in local communities. No wonder they're less safe."

Peter saw Reverend Howard waving to him and said, "Here comes Reverend Howard with Earl Price." The reverend introduced Ruth to his friend and explained that Earl would be researching the center and interviewing the employees and the residents. Ruth surmised that Earl Price was an author and was gathering information for a book.

"Peter, would you show Earl around while I visit with Ruth?"

When Peter and Earl were out of earshot, the reverend said, "Peter speaks well of you, Ruth, both in the way that you handle yourself and in the way that you tend to your duties here."

"Peter is congenial, and I appreciate the help he has given me."

"I have noticed that you play the piano beautifully, Ruth. I have proposed to Peter that we add music to our worship service here, and we were wondering if we could make use of your musical talent."

"What do you have in mind?"

"Some hymn singing, with you at the piano, and perhaps a prelude and a postlude of your choice."

"I would be happy to do that," she responded.

He asked if she would also be willing to prepare a program of piano selections of her choice for a monthly recital in the lounge.

"Well," she said, "that would require my practicing the piano often, and some of the residents might find that disturbing."

"There are other places here that a resident can go for relaxation or meditation, Ruth."

"That's what my mother said. She is worried that I will lose my skills if I don't practice enough." She paused. "I can play for the worship service this Sunday, but I would want to practice for a month before a recital."

"Fine, Ruth. I look forward to it. I see that Peter and Earl have returned." He excused himself.

While Ruth and Reverend Howard were visiting, she noticed that Judy was intently watching them. As soon as he excused himself, Judy approached Ruth. "Can I share something with you that might need Reverend Howard's attention?" Judy asked. Ruth invited Judy to sit down. "Do you know my son, Jacob?"

"No. I've noticed him when he comes to visit you, but I've not been introduced to him. Tell me about him, Judy."

"He's a wonderful son," she began. "I'm proud of him. My husband Carl and I raised him to be good, but he didn't need much guidance. We gave him all of the advantages of wealth, and he could have become arrogant and self-centered, but he remained unspoiled.

Carl and I took him everywhere with us: Europe, Canada, Australia, South America, Asia – everywhere but the moon." Ruth laughed. "Jacob did well in school and was admitted to Princeton, Carl's alma mater. Unlike many college students, he didn't become discontented, cynical, or radical. He emerged from college a sensible, good-hearted young man. Five years later, he met and married Adelaide, who has been a fine addition to the family. They have a successful marriage and two beautiful children."

"That's a glowing description," remarked Ruth.

"One thing more," Judy continued. "Jacob is the trustee of our estate, and I have no complaints about his handling of it. He keeps me well-informed, but Evan constantly tries to interest Jacob in a vacation home – first in the Banff area of Canada, then in the area of Aspen, Colorado, and now in the Lake Tahoe area. Jacob doesn't want to get involved with a private venture of Evan's."

"What do you want me to do, Judy?"

"You're a friend of Evan's. Can you find out about this business venture of his?"

"I can't get involved in his personal affairs, but I'll stay alert to the situation."

When Judy left, Ruth went up to her study to record their conversation in Judy's folder. Judy had seemed to Ruth like a mother bear who senses danger and is ready to protect her cub. Judy and Jacob appeared to be suspicious of Evan, and Judy was beginning to take action. From Judy's past record, it was obvious to Ruth that as the wife of a wealthy man, she had involved herself in charitable organizations and had sometimes taken a leadership role. Ruth wrote: *Judy likes to be in charge.*

Ruth did not record her personal thoughts about Evan: She reasoned that, like Judy, he is involved in charities, his mission and the animal shelter, but he continually needs to seek funds to operate them, whereas Judy and Jacob already have their wealth. *I'd better be careful not to get involved or to cast suspicion on Evan,* she thought. *Let it sort itself out.*

Chapter XIX: Lake Tahoe

Towards the end of the week, Mrs. Martin called Ruth.

"Could you come home this weekend?" she asked. "A very festive choral concert is taking place in the chapel at Santa Clara University, and Dad and I are going. We have extra tickets. Would you and Peter like to go with us?"

"Peter has never invited me out. I don't think that I should invite him."

"Don't be a stickler about that, Ruth. If you want him to come, ask him."

"No, Mom. He just returned from an emergency trip to Tucson. His father was in a bad car accident."

"Was he badly hurt?"

"Yes, but he is on the way to recovery. Peter is back but has a lot of catching up to do. I'll ask Evan instead."

"O.K., Ruth. Evan is welcome to be our guest for the weekend."

***

When Ruth invited Evan, he declined, saying that he had a business meeting with an associate in Santa Cruz. However, the following weekend he would be free and was planning to go to Lake Tahoe to visit with his friend, Willie, who has a cabin in the Sierra Nevada Mountains. "Would you like to go with me, Ruth? We could either stay overnight with Willie or in a hotel at South Lake Tahoe. Your choice."

Ruth said that she preferred the hotel. "I'll see how my schedule works out," she responded, "and let you know on Friday." Ruth called her mother once she had decided to go and told her that she was going with Evan for a weekend trip to Lake Tahoe. "We'll be staying at a hotel at South Lake Tahoe. I don't know which one yet, but it will probably be a casino hotel."

"A casino hotel? You don't like to gamble, Ruth."

"We're going for the scenery, Mom, and Evan is meeting with a friend there."

"Well, don't let Evan drive too fast, and call us when you're back."

***

As the following weekend approached, Evan informed Ruth that they would be leaving at 6:00 a.m. "We'll stop for coffee and something to eat when we get to Placerville," he explained. "Bring along your swim suit. There is a pool at the casino, and there will be a dinner show in the evening." Ruth packed a small bag with swim suit, a dress and heels, pajamas, and toiletries.

Rather than heading directly for Highway 5 on Saturday morning, Evan drove through a maze of single and narrow two-lane canal roads.

Ruth finally asked, "Where are we?"

"Close to Rio Vista. There's a bridge coming up that will take us to Highway 5. I thought you might be interested in seeing the vegetation along the canals."

"I am." She pointed. "Look at that canal! It's so dense with flowers, you wouldn't be able to get through by boat."

"Yes. They would choke the engine," responded Evan.

"The flowers are glorious. What are those plants?"

"The plants with floating green pods and white flowers are sponge plants. They grow fast, but not as rapidly as the water hyacinth, the ones with purple, showy blossoms."

"What a mat of bright color – so beautiful!"

"But destructive to other vegetation in the area. They are the fastest growing plant in the **world**, Ruth! A single plant can cover 6,500 square feet of water per year, with floating mats six feet deep. They choke out all other vegetation."

"Why are they allowed to grow?"

"They are so aggressive, they can only be contained, but never eradicated."

"It just shows you that some things can be beautiful on the outside and destructive on the inside."

Once over the bridge, Evan increased his speed as he headed to Highway 5 towards Sacramento, where he turned onto Highway 50. In the old forty-niner gold rush town of Placerville, he stopped at a bakery-café where they had coffee and freshly baked cinnamon rolls. From there to Stateline (bordering Nevada), the highway gradually ascended into the Sierra Nevada Mountains. Arriving at the casino, Evan informed Ruth that it was too early to check in, but his friend Willie was waiting in the coffee shop.

Willie rose from his seat when he saw Evan and Ruth approaching. Evan introduced Willie to Ruth: "Willie Socorro, this is Ruth Martin from the center."

"Hi, there, Ruth," Willie responded. "We can put your bags in my jeep for now. Before we leave for the cabin, you might want to use the restroom. We're going to be on Route 89, the Emerald Bay Road for several hours. Route 89 goes entirely around the lake, and my cabin is halfway around. The route there is scenic, with plenty of pull-outs where we can stop to see the vistas. Unfortunately, there is just an occasional porta potty; so, it is best to go here where you can wash up."

En route, they had spectacular views of the lake, with the exception of the areas where the forest hid the lake. As they headed north, the lake was on their right, and stretches of trees, rocky outcroppings, and an occasional waterfall on their left.

An hour and a half later, Willie turned onto a one-lane dirt and gravel road which followed a ravine until they reached a clearing in the trees.

"I can see why you need a jeep," commented Ruth, as they pulled into the clearing. The log cabin sat atop a slight rise in the land. Willie parked and led them up wooden steps and across a plank deck.

"Welcome!" he said, as he opened the door. They stepped into a large room with a beamed ceiling and log walls. To one side of the room was a kitchenette with oven and stove, a refrigerator, open shelves for dishes and supplies, and a counter with four stools. On the other side, a circular metal staircase led to sleeping quarters in an open loft. Under the loft were an enclosed bedroom and bathroom. On the concrete floor of the cabin lay rag rugs. A big stone fireplace dominated the room. Couches on either side of the fireplace provided extra sleeping spots when needed.

"Charming," complimented Ruth.

"Thanks," said Willie. "Why don't you two go out to the deck and enjoy the trees and the birds? I'll get a fire going in the fireplace and set out some bread, cheese, and cold cuts for lunch." While on the deck, Evan explained to Ruth that Willie had built the cabin himself.

During lunch, Evan asked Willie how many plots of land he had for sale now. "Four plots, and I have several interested buyers," he answered. Evan explained to Ruth that Willie sells unimproved land to clients who want to build a vacation home. After purchasing land from the E & W Land Developers, clients can hire their own contractor to build a home, or Willie can build it. Evan added, "Willie can do any kind of manual labor." Willie nodded and patted himself on the back.

"Ruth," Evan said, "your parents might be interested in a vacation home like this."

"It would be pretty remote for them. Just getting here would not be easy."

"Helicopters exist, Ruth. If the plot of land were big enough, a large spacious clearing would solve that problem."

"My father is a very busy man, Evan. He seldom vacations except when he combines it with a business trip."

Evan seemed annoyed with her response. Turning to Willie, he said, "Shall we go into your bedroom to discuss business?"

"O.K.," Willie answered and invited Ruth to make herself at home, either inside or out on the deck. When the meeting was over, Willie drove them back to the hotel, took their bags inside, promised to keep in touch with Evan, and said goodbye. Evan suggested to Ruth that she have a swim before dinner and, perhaps, a nap afterward, while he has some work to do. "Meet me at 8:00 p.m. in the Steak and Chop House. We'll go to the dinner show."

Ruth had her swim and then went to her room. From the picture window, she had a picturesque view of the lake and the mountains; she turned on T.V. to a music station and rested until dinner time.

Dinner at the restaurant was excellent. Evan ordered a bottle of brut champagne with the meal, and they enjoyed the entertainment of the stand-up comic. As they separated for the night, Evan said, "I'll be working late tonight, so I will want to 'sleep in' tomorrow morning. Feel free, Ruth, to have breakfast in the coffee shop and then go to the spa afterward or go for another swim. We'll check out at 2:00 p.m. I'll meet you in the lobby. Sleep well."

"Thanks, Evan. Good luck with your work."

Ruth didn't see Evan until close to 2:00 p.m. in the lobby for check-out. While he was waiting for the clerk, a young lady approached him and said jovially, "Did you finally call it quits last night?" He smiled, shrugged, and turned to the clerk.

"What was that all about?" Ruth asked.

"I have no idea. She must have had me confused with someone else."

On the drive home, they conversed infrequently; Evan was on the speaker phone occasionally, and Ruth was lost in thought. When Ruth reached the center, she called her mother to let her know that she had arrived back safely.

"How was your time with Evan?" her mother asked.

"The scenery was lovely. Except for the drive, Evan and I didn't see much of each other. He always seemed to have work to do and needed to be by himself. I don't think that Evan is really interested in me, Mom."

"Perhaps you're right about that."

"Why, Mom?"

"Last weekend when you invited him here, he said that he couldn't come because he had a business meeting with an associate in Santa Cruz."

"Yes, that's what he said."

"Well, Dad and I went to the Crow's Nest in Santa Cruz for a fish dinner on Saturday, and we saw Evan there with a young woman who was not dressed for a business meeting."

"Did he see you?"

"No. You know how the restaurant is set up, with inside seating areas and tables under heat lamps outside. Evan had his back to us, and the woman was facing the window towards us. She was wearing a short, tight skirt, a low-cut blouse, and 5" heels. They appeared to be having an intimate time, laughing and reaching out to each other."

"I get the picture, Mom. I'll see what I can find out about it."

"Hold off until the time seems right to inquire, Ruth."

***

Several days later, Ruth was having lunch in the garden when Evan and Earl Price came over to her table. "Here's my girlfriend, Ruth," Evan said to Earl. Earl responded that he and Ruth were acquainted. Ruth frowned and corrected Evan, explaining that she and Evan were just friends. "Evan has just been telling me about your trip to Tahoe, Ruth. Did you win or lose?" asked Earl.

"Neither. I don't gamble. We went to Lake Tahoe for the scenery. I found it peaceful and beautiful." When Earl saw Peter approaching, he left to talk with him. Ruth turned to Evan and chided him for calling her his girlfriend.

"Isn't that what you are?" he asked.

"If so, I'm one of several."

"What do you mean, Ruth?"

"You were seen at the Crow's Nest with your business associate, having a romantic time together."

"By your parents, I guess. Well, you can tell them that we are co-owners of a start-up movie company, and we were making a trailer with a romantic scene for an upcoming movie."

"Where were the cameras?"

"They were there. Your spies - excuse me, your parents - just didn't see them. You know, Ruth, jealousy doesn't become you."

Ruth's face reddened as she hastily got up and walked away. She noticed that Peter and Earl had been watching them. Ruth went to her apartment and put on a CD of soft music. Once she had composed herself, she got out her notes and turned her attention to the upcoming circle meeting.

A few hours later, Ruth came into the lounge with an armful of piano music. She chose a Chopin waltz to brighten up her spirit.

Peter, who had been in the library, came in to listen. When Ruth finished the piece, he asked her if she was feeling better.

"Yes. I was annoyed and embarrassed with what Evan said to Earl Price and then to me. My personal life is not Evan's to share."

"Don't worry about Earl. He is beginning to know what Evan is like."

"Peter, I'd like to share with you something about Evan." Peter nodded and invited Ruth to sit with him on the couch.

"Evan invited me to Lake Tahoe for the weekend. We had separate rooms (my choice) at a casino hotel (his choice). I needn't have worried about a romantic set-up because his goal was to interest me in a plot of land for a vacation home. He wanted me to talk to my parents about purchasing land. He took me to see his friend's cabin in the mountains. I explained that a cabin in such a remote area wouldn't be suitable for my family and me."

"Then that should be the end of it. Are you concerned about his trying to sell you real estate?"

"No. However, according to Judy, Evan has been pressuring her son Jacob to buy a plot of land for a vacation home, and Jacob is getting fed up with it. Judy wanted me to look into it."

"I see. Let me handle it, Ruth. I will bring it to Reverend Howard's attention." He paused and then added, "Ruth, as far as spending the weekend with Evan, there are no rules here about dating."

"O.K., Peter."

"And Ruth?" They looked directly at each other. "I think that Evan missed an opportunity to get to know you better."

Chapter XX: The Fall from Creation

Ruth put her concerns about Evan behind her as she prepared for the discussion group meeting on Monday afternoon. The morning of the meeting, she took a walk along the canal to ease her nervousness. Following lunch in the garden, she entered the library and waited for the group to assemble.

"As we begin our study and discussion today," Ruth began, "let's review what we have learned in 'Genesis 1 and 2': God started with a spiritual idea and formed it into matter. God first created light and the expanse of the universe, including many solar systems; then He created **our** solar system, including the earth and its atmosphere, water, and land; and in the water, the creatures of the seas; and on the land, the plants and the birds and the animals. His creation culminated with man, whom He created in His own image, a being with a mind and soul.   At each stage of His creation, God pronounced it good. He had created a universe in which the different elements were orderly and worked together in harmony: the suns ruled the planets and moons within their own solar systems, and our sun and moon in our solar system ruled the earth. To man, God gave dominion over the plants and the animal kingdom, along with the duty to provide and care for them. For happiness, He gave Adam a garden as a home and ordered him to tend it. He then created a helpmate for Adam, for companionship and procreation. At this point, Eve entered the story. That's where we continue the story today.

"I would like to follow this format in our study today: Cindy will read from her Bible different sections of the text as you follow along with your own version of the Bible. Then we will discuss the text, incorporating meaning from the different versions. Hopefully, we will end up with a rich understanding of the text. After Cindy has read a section, I will call on one of you to paraphrase it from your Bible; then I will elicit comments and questions from the group.

"Please turn to Genesis, Chapter 2, Verses 21 through 25. In my text, this section is called 'The Creation of Woman.' Cindy, please begin."

When Cindy finished reading, Ruth called on Judy to paraphrase the text from her Bible.

Judy: "God thinks that it isn't good for Adam to be alone, so He makes a mate for him from one of Adam's ribs. God takes the mate to Adam, who names her 'woman.' Adam and the woman are spiritually without sin and physically naked, but without shame."

Ruth: "Why do you think that God wanted Adam to have a mate?"

Ralph: "To have a lover and soulmate."

Dr. Sandler: "To become fruitful and multiply, like the other creatures."

Gloria: "To help each other take care of the garden."

Ruth: "Genesis, Chapter 3, verses 1 through 6 describe the serpent tempting Eve to disobey God's command not to eat the fruit from the tree in the middle of the garden." Following Cindy's reading, Ruth asked Ralph to paraphrase it.

Ralph: "The serpent wants to destroy Adam and Eve and the garden. He chooses to tempt Eve rather than Adam. He says that she will not die if she eats from the tree of good and evil. Instead, she will become wise, like God. Eve finds the fruit very appealing, and she disobeys God's order not to eat and then gives some of the fruit to Adam to eat."

Ruth: "Why do you think that the serpent wants to destroy God's creation?"

Oscar: "Hatred for God."

Gloria: "Envy, jealousy of God."

Elizabeth: "Revenge. God expelled Satan from Heaven because Satan had led a rebellion against God."

Ruth: "How does the serpent show his wiliness in his conversation with Eve?"

Judy: "First of all, by approaching Eve instead of Adam. I think that the serpent judges Eve to be weaker than Adam."

Oscar: "I think that he considers Adam to be more intelligent."

Ralph chuckled. The women showed their disapproval of Oscar's remark by their body language.

Elizabeth: "The serpent twisted God's words. God had warned Adam and Eve: 'Do not eat of **the tree of good and evil;** if you do, you will **surely die**.' The serpent changed that to 'You shall not eat of **every tree** in the garden, but if you do, you **won't die**.' Eve then hands the fruit to Adam, who does not challenge Eve's disobedience, but joins her in eating the forbidden fruit. They both immediately know good from evil and realize that they are naked and are ashamed."

Ruth: "Cindy, please read verses 8 through 13." Ruth then asked Gloria to paraphrase the section.

Gloria: "God comes looking for them in the garden. When He finds them, He asks Adam how he knew that he was naked. Adam blames God for bringing Eve to him; in other words, for **creating** Eve, who has tempted him and gotten them into trouble. Eve responds by saying, 'It's not my fault; the serpent tempted me.'"

Ruth: "What do you learn about Adam from his not challenging Eve about her disobedience?"

Oscar: "That he is weak and unwilling to 'wear the pants in their relationship.'"

Ruth: "Why does God come looking for them in the garden? He knows where they are and why they're hiding."

Elizabeth: "He wants to give them a chance to confess their sin, but instead, they try to explain away their wrong doing by blaming each other and by blaming even God Himself."

"Cindy, please read Verses 14 through 20." Ruth then asked Dr. Sandler to paraphrase it.

Dr. Sandler: "God curses the serpent and declares him the lowliest of creatures. Then God prophesies that the serpent (i.e., Satan) will be destroyed in the end by goodness. This will come about after Christ is born into the human race, undergoes suffering on the cross, and delivers a death blow to Satan: Christ will overcome death when He is resurrected. God then punishes Adam and Eve for their disobedience. He pronounces that the gates of the garden will be locked so that they can never eat from the tree of life, which is located in the center of the garden. If they were to eat of this tree, it would give them eternal life. Instead, they are to have only mortal life and will eventually experience physical death and decay, dust returning to dust. On earth, Adam will toil and labor throughout his mortal life, and Eve will experience the pangs of childbirth. Thus, sin and death and suffering entered paradise. Eternal life will only be possible to mankind through divine intervention."

Ruth: "Verse 15 contains what is called the first Messianic prophecy." Ruth reread the verse aloud, emphasizing the words *enmity, seed, heel, bruise.* "Can anyone explain the meaning of the prophecy?" Ruth asked.

Elizabeth answered: "It's symbolic. God promises that in the end, evil will be destroyed (enmity between good and evil). The Messiah (Christ) will be born of woman (i.e. the seed of the human race) and conceived by the Holy Spirit. Sin and death will be conquered through Christ's sacrifice on the cross (the bruising of Christ's heel symbolizes his suffering on the cross in order to crush Satan's head, that is, to destroy Satan. Thus, Christ's death and resurrection are the **divine intervention** that mankind needs to regain **eternal life**."

Ruth: "From this point, 'Genesis' becomes less symbolic in language and more narrative. The story of Adam and Eve, as father and mother of mankind, continues with the generations that follow. As we close this symbolic part of 'Genesis,' what are your questions or comments?"

Judy: "To me, 'Genesis' explains why God allows evil, illness, and death in the world."

Dr. Sandler: "Yes. C.S. Lewis in his book, *The Problem of Pain*, explains that good gets its full meaning from being the opposite of pain. Our life on earth is full of opposites: sickness vs. health, happiness vs. sadness, life vs. death."

Elizabeth: "God is an immortal being. With our mortal minds, we can only catch a glimpse of the mind of God. No matter how erudite we become, we are like amoebas, trying to study hard to become Einsteins."

Oscar: "Good one, Elizabeth!" She smiled. "What strikes me," he continued, "is how smart the devil is in his attempt to destroy God's creation."

Ruth: "Remember our discussion about the devil's cleverness and power. The devil has superior intelligence and ability to ours."

Oscar: "I remember, 'Don't let the devil get his foot in the door.'"

Peter: "The devil is a **spiritual** being but not a <u>**self-existent being**</u>, as the Creator is. As C.S. Lewis said in *The Preface to Paradise Lost*, **'Only a self-existent being can understand its own existence; a created being merely finds itself existing**.' I believe that angels and devils are **created** spiritual beings, and that there is only one **God, one <u>self-existent</u> being**, who understands Himself and all that He created. As far as **our** understanding how matter came about, we are learning more all the time about space and time and about the laws of the universe, but no matter how much we learn, we will never be able to explain <u>**self-existence**</u>.

Oscar: "The old saying is true: It takes one to know one."

Ruth: "Thank you, Peter, for your insight, and thanks to all of you for sharing your thoughts."

As they were leaving the library, Peter said to Ruth, "A beautifully thought-out discussion, Ruth."

"Thanks. I hope that I didn't sow any seeds of doubt."

"On the contrary."

Ruth asked Peter if he wanted to have coffee with her, but he declined and apologized, saying that he had meetings in the afternoon with Reverend Howard and then with Earl Price. After dinner, the three would meet again in the reverend's office, and their meeting might last well into the evening. Ruth did not press Peter for information; instead, she went to the chapel to think over the group meeting.

Chapter XXI: Peter's Mission

Ruth was in her pajamas, robe, and slippers when there was a knock at the door to her apartment. It was Peter. "May I come in?" he asked. Ruth invited him in and asked if he would like a glass of sherry.

"Yes. I won't stay long. I've been with Reverend Howard and Earl all evening. We have reached a decision in regard to a very delicate situation here at the center. Reverend has asked me to take on a mission to help him to begin legal action."

"Does this involve Evan or me?" Ruth asked.

"Yes, it involves Evan, but I am not at liberty to tell you any details at this time. You aren't involved directly in the issue other than in communicating with me."

"I don't understand, Peter."

"The first part of the mission assigned to me is to take a leave of absence here until the situation is resolved. I have decided to take a trip to the Banff area in Canada. I have always wanted to see the Canadian Rockies. I have asked Reverend Howard if it will be alright if I communicate with you while I am away, and he has allowed me to do that."

"When are you leaving, Peter?"

"In two days. I'm sorry about the secrecy, but everything will eventually get cleared up. Since I will be gone for a while, I was wondering if you might be able to spend the whole day tomorrow with me. We always seem to have just a few hours here and there, and I would like to get to know you better. No meetings or business, just 'hanging out,' starting with coffee in the garden."

"I would like that, Peter. What time?"

"Meet me at 9:00 a.m. on the patio. I'll bring the coffee, and we can plan our day together."

When Peter left, Ruth called her mother and filled her in on the latest developments in her personal life. Mrs. Martin agreed that Evan was obviously under suspicion at the center and that Peter apparently was reaching out to Ruth with romantic interest. "It sounds like Peter needs and wants your support, Ruth," she said. "Spending the day together will enable you to get to know him better, too. Now that Evan is under suspicion, perhaps Peter feels freer to show a desire to get to know you.

***

In the morning, Ruth dressed in khaki pants and a gold-colored blouse with white lace trim around the neckline. (*The gold color will draw attention to my hazel eyes*, she thought. *One of my better features*.)

Peter was waiting in the garden with a container of coffee, two cups, and cinnamon rolls. "I thought we might leisurely plan our day over a cup of coffee," Peter said as he poured a cup for Ruth. "We can take turns making suggestions. First, I suggest that we sit here after our rolls for a second cup of coffee and a game of Scrabble."

"I love Scrabble, Peter. How about a walk afterward?"

"Good. And we can have lunch back here in the garden."

"Followed by a short boat ride. I'll help with the rowing, Peter."

"For the afternoon, how about a DVD to watch either in your apartment or mine? You can choose from my DVD collection, Ruth."

"O.K., but you'll be stuck with my choice."

"I get the last suggestion," said Peter. "Following a brief rest and change of clothes, I'd like to take you to dinner at Wine and Roses in Lodi. O.K.?"

"I love that place," Ruth remarked with enthusiasm.

The game of Scrabble went well. Peter had brought an egg timer, which he set for each play – three minutes per turn; it kept the game moving along. They were equally skilled, but Peter played all of his tiles at one point and ended up winning. For their walk, they chose a path outside of the garden, starting behind the chapel; they rested briefly inside the chapel on their return.

Their next activity was lunch in the dining room. "Do you feel like today's Greek salad?" Peter asked. "Yes, I like salad for lunch, especially when I'm being taken to dinner later by a charming companion." Peter gave her a quick wink. "Greek salad, it is."

Before pushing off from the boat dock following lunch, Peter warned that he was not an expert at following the maze of canals. "However," he stated, "I know a few landmarks to follow to a small island just a short distance away."

"Aye, aye, captain," Ruth responded. After a few instructions from Peter, they rowed smoothly together. They enjoyed the water, the seagulls flying overhead, and the vegetation along the banks of the canal. Without stopping, they encircled the island and returned to home base.

"Let's go to my apartment, where you can look through my DVDs," said Peter. Ruth paged through a catalog he had created and selected *Brigadoon* with Gene Kelly, Cyd Charisse, and Van Johnson. "I love the music in this film," remarked Ruth, "and the central message."

"Remind me of the message," Peter said.

"If you love someone deeply enough, anything is possible," Ruth answered.

When the movie was over, Peter said, "Tommy Albright, the main character, gave up an excellent job, money, and the advantages of the modern world for a humble life back in the 17th century, to be with the girl he loves – Fiona. His decision illustrates that we need **faith** to find happiness and love because believing requires more than just witnessing with one's eyes."

"Yes," agreed Ruth. "On the surface, *Brigadoon* is a fairy tale, but its message is spiritual."

Peter paraphrased his favorite line from the film: "It's the hardest thing in the world to **give** up everything, but it's usually the only way to **get** everything." Ruth nodded and Peter continued, "I'll come to get you in an hour, Ruth, after you've had a chance to freshen up and change for dinner."

For the evening, Ruth wore a mint-green silk dress with black pumps. Peter was attired in light gray. From Highway 5, they turned onto Turner Road and drove past several wineries on their way to Wine and Roses. At the restaurant, to the left of the parking lot was a stunning circular garden of red, purple, pink, and white Dutch ranunculus; yellow and white daffodils, and tall blue anemones. "Let's go into the tasting room and get goblets of wine to drink here in this garden," suggested Peter.

"We always seem to be headed for a garden," said Ruth. After the wine, they walked along a gravel path bordered by more flowers and low bushes. The restaurant was located in a renovated farm house. They entered a lounge, which had a fireplace and a bar. Several small rooms off the lounge provided an intimate indoor space for dinner, and the deck outside offered a pastoral ambience.

Peter pointed and said, "Look out there past the lawn, Ruth. Under that trellis, a lot of marriages take place. I've attended a few here at which Reverend Howard has officiated."

"This is an ideal location for an outdoor wedding," she acknowledged.

It was 10:00 p.m. when they arrived back at the center. "Wait a second, Ruth, before we say goodnight. Let's sit here by the fireplace. I may not have another chance to talk with you before I leave." Ruth nodded. He explained that he had made reservations at Emerald Lake in Alberta, Canada and that he would like to communicate with her by email while he was gone. "Would that be O.K. with you, Ruth?"

"I'd like that, Peter." He took her hand and looked into her eyes. "I've had a wonderful day with you, Ruth. It was just the way I had imagined it."

"Well, we planned it together. It had to turn out well, didn't it?"

"**Just** well?"

"**Very** well." Peter escorted her to her apartment, took her key, and opened her door for her. As she took a step forward, he reached out for her, hugged her tightly, and kissed her on the neck. "I knew you'd smell good," he whispered.

***

Peter emailed her from Canada two days later.

<u>Peter to Ruth</u>: How are you? What's new there? Is Evan still around? I wish you were here. It is so beautiful; the lake is a gorgeous emerald-green color, which is caused by the minerals in the water from the melting of the nearby glaciers. The water is ice cold. I took a rowboat out yesterday but was careful not to fall in. Until later, Peter

<u>Ruth to Peter</u>: Hi, Peter. Evan is still here. I saw him having lunch with his grandmother yesterday. He's finally spending some time with her. Earl has been here all day. I saw him with Ralph before lunch and then with Oscar after lunch. Emerald Lake sounds beautiful. Are there cabins there or a lodge or both? Stay warm. Ruth

<u>Peter to Ruth</u>: Dear Ruth, I wish you were here. Today I walked completely around the lake, about 3/4th mile in circumference. Seeing the lake from different viewpoints was delightful. Yes, there is a lodge here, but it is only for a common room, a restaurant, and office space. The sleeping quarters are all in individual cabins. What's new? Reverend Howard keeps faxing me papers to study. Please try to avoid meeting with Evan or any of the members of the circle group. Stay safe. Peter

<u>Ruth to Peter</u>: Hi, Peter. You have me worried. I am staying clear of Evan and keeping a low profile with the group, especially Oscar, Judy, and Gloria. I noticed that Judy met with Reverend Howard today, but I managed to avoid her. Is it safe to walk around the lake? If a bear came along, you wouldn't want to try to escape into the ice-cold water. Be careful. Ruth

<u>Peter to Ruth</u>: Dear Ruth, I'm glad you're concerned about me. I'm equally worried about you. Until there is a resolution to this God-awful mess, I'll feel ill at ease. I hope that Judy doesn't try to handle things herself. A professional is needed. On a lighter note, I drove to the Lake Louise area today and took the chairlift up the mountain. From the top, there was a breathtaking view of the lake. It was the best day I've had since 'our day' together! I miss you! Peter

<u>Ruth to Peter</u>: Dear Peter, my news today is about Gloria. I saw her only briefly with Evan. They were coming back to the center from 'somewhere.' Gloria was sobbing, and Evan looked angry and anxious. I know that Gloria needs help, but I can't reach out to her in this situation. I hope that Reverend Howard will soon take action. You're right about the Lake Louise area being idyllic. My parents took me there on vacation when I was twelve. Emerald Lake, however, sounds like less of a tourist site. I can picture you more in that secluded spot. I hope you come back soon. Ruth

<u>Peter to Ruth</u>: Dear Ruth, the situation at the center should be resolved soon. Reverend Howard wants me to return, suggesting that a solution to the 'Evan problem' is imminent. But for the time being, please stay clear of Evan. I will be home in a day or two. I am anxious to see you. I hope that we can pick up where we left off. Yours, Peter

<u>Ruth to Peter</u>: Dear Peter, travel safely. You are in my thoughts and prayers. I remember 'our day' together. Yours, Ruth

Chapter XXII: Evan Revealed

Two days later, Edith informed Ruth that Reverend Howard would like to meet with her in his office after dinner. When she entered, she could see that he was upset.

"Bad news," he announced. "Evan has left without notice."

"Oh! When?"

"We're not sure. Edith was trying to keep an eye on him. No one saw him move out. He must have left during the night. Edith searched his room. He left behind only some library books. He was careful to clear out his desk and go through his trash, taking any scraps of evidence with him."

"Who knows about his leaving?"

"Only Edith, Earl, you and I. I've tried to reach Peter, but he must be traveling. Evan's grandmother is very worried about Evan; she can't reach him."

"I'm not surprised. He has not treated her well."

"I'm afraid that I have waited too long to take steps," said Reverend Howard. "I've been waiting for Earl to complete his investigation and his report; he feels that it will be ready when Peter comes home tomorrow."

"Is there anything I can do in the meantime?" asked Ruth.

"Yes. Offer words of comfort to Gloria, but don't discuss Evan with her."

The following morning, Ruth awoke early, keyed up for the day ahead. She stayed in bed for an hour listening to Vivaldi's *Four Seasons* before arising. When she went down to the dining room, she joined Dr. Sandler for breakfast.

"Good morning, Ruth. Is it going to be another crazy day?"

"I guess we'll find out," she responded. He discreetly changed the subject, asking her if she would be playing the piano this morning. When they finished their breakfast, Ruth went into the lounge to play, and Dr. Sandler followed to listen. After an hour, Ruth went to Edith's office to find out when Peter would be returning.

"He has already returned, Ruth – about 9:00 a.m. this morning."

"How did he look?" Ruth asked.

"Scruffy, like he's been living in an airport. He went to his apartment to shower and shave and change clothes. He left this message for you." The message read: Ruth, *meet me in the chapel at 2:00 p.m. Peter*

When Peter entered the chapel, Ruth was waiting. From behind his back, he brought forward a bouquet of red roses and white daisies, saying, "For you, Ruth. I bought these at the airport."

"That was very thoughtful of you, Peter." She got a vase from a niche, filled it with water from a spigot, and set the vase on a stand back in the niche. "They're for **you**, Ruth," Peter complained.

"Yes, thank you, but I want to share them with others. Don't worry; I'll be back several times a day to visit them." Peter laughed. "It's two hours until the meeting with Reverend Howard. Let's go for a walk," he suggested.

They left the chapel through a door to the path they had taken during 'their day together.' After just a few feet, Peter took hold of Ruth's hand and pulled her towards him. "I can't wait any longer," he said, embracing her and kissing her on the neck and then the cheek and then the lips. "I love you, Ruth," he said, holding her closely.

"I've been wanting to hear you say that for some time, Peter." They held hands as they walked along the path behind the chapel, which eventually wound its way to the front of the building. As they entered the building, Cindy was sitting in the lobby. She watched them as they went to their mailboxes and retrieved their mail. She heard Peter murmur to Ruth as they parted.

At 4:00 p.m. Ruth met with Reverend Howard, Earl, Peter, and Edith, who had come prepared to take notes. Reverend Howard began. "You all realize by now that Earl is not only a friend but a police detective." They nodded. "His investigation has given sufficient evidence of Evan's dishonest money-making schemes. Earl has taken the evidence to the district attorney, who has begun proceedings against Evan. Evan has been served with a subpoena to appear in court, but he has ignored it and has fled. The police now have a warrant out for his arrest."

"What are the charges against him?" asked Peter.

Earl read from the top sheet of papers that he had brought with him: (1) Soliciting funds for God's Bounty Mission in Oakland and improperly using them. The operation of the mission has included Emile Romero, his wife, and Evan.

(2) Soliciting funds for the E & J Pet Shelter in Sacramento and improperly using them. The operation has involved Evan and Oscar's son, Jake Oliver.

(3) An investment scam by the E& W Land Developers for the sale of unimproved, non-existent plots of land near Lake Tahoe. The operation has involved Evan and his friend, Willie Socorro.

Not included in the indictment is an attempt to start a company to make movie trailers for films. That involved a young woman in San Jose. Since money has not yet changed hands, there is no proof of intent to defraud.

At this point, Reverend Howard entered the discourse. "Thank you, Earl, for a thorough job of investigation. Thank you, Peter, for participating in a mission to bring about justice. Thank you, Edith, for keeping good financial records and for your attention to detail. Ruth, thank you for responding with sensitivity to our residents."

Peter spoke up. "Thank you, Reverend, for **your** leadership." The others nodded.

"Unfortunately," continued the reverend, "Evan has left quite a few victims, who responded financially to his schemes. Our institution here has been hurt in various ways: our reputation, our finances, and our need to make restitution to the residents who have been affected by Evan's dishonesty. My biggest concern going forward is not the money, but the welfare of the residents. Gloria, Ralph, and Oscar have all suffered both financial loss and disgrace relating to their children."

"Reverend, we can all help you with emotional help for the residents," Peter offered.

"Thank you. On that positive note, let us close with prayer," concluded the reverend.

Following the meeting, Peter and Ruth walked to the dock, where they sat on the bench to watch the ducks and listen to the lapping of the water against the dock. "Peaceful here, isn't it?" asked Ruth.

"Yes, water restores."

"Peter, I'm concerned about Oscar, Ralph and Gloria."

"Oscar was already used to Jake's behavior. You've heard him call Jake a bum. In Oscar's eyes, Jake had already tarnished the Oliver name. I don't think that Ralph will suffer that much from embarrassment either, but Gloria will definitely need our help."

"Did she lose a lot of her money?" asked Ruth.

"A substantial amount. She probably has enough left to live comfortably on, but she may not want the disgrace of living here. She is a proud woman and will not want sympathy."

"Do you think that she will want to seek retribution from Evan?"

"I doubt it. She made the investments with him willingly. Besides, she would find a trial humiliating. Evan's betrayal of her will be hard for her to reconcile. After all, she raised him and loved him."

"That is the worst blow of all."

"I looked at her records," said Peter. "She has no blood relatives, but her husband Roger had a sister in Madison, Nebraska who is still living. The sister is about Gloria's age, a widow with two children, a nephew and niece to Gloria. Gloria might want to return to Nebraska, where she and Roger grew up, graduated from the University of Nebraska, and married before moving to the west coast."

"Perhaps we can help her to find a way forward, Peter. From a discussion I had with her when you were in Tucson, she confided that she felt guilty about not having been able to be an adequate mother to Evan when Evangeline died. Gloria will need encouragement to not blame herself for Evan's criminality."

"You're right, and you're sweet, Ruth."

Before Ruth retired for the night, she called her mother to report on the events that had taken place since they last spoke. Ruth told her mother about 'spending the day' with Peter. (Mrs. Martin thought that Peter had been clever in planning it with Ruth.) Next, she told her mother about the meeting with Reverend Howard and Evan's investment schemes. (Mrs. Martin was not surprised.) Finally, Ruth explained that Evan was evading the police, who had a warrant out for his arrest.

"Ruth, I didn't like Evan from the beginning, and my gut feeling about him seems to have been correct," she remarked. "Thank God he is out of your life, and thank God for Peter."

"You know, Mom, Peter is a sweet, romantic man. He's spiritual, considerate, sensitive, caring - --"

117

"In other words, he is perfect for you. I think that it's time for Dad and me to get to know him. Come home for the weekend, and bring him with you, Ruthie."

Chapter XXIII: The Martins

On Saturday, Peter drove Ruth's car as they left for the Martin home in Los Gatos. They took coffee with them to sip along the way. Near the intersection of Highway 580 and Highway 680, they headed towards Livermore. Ruth advised Peter to go through Livermore for a scenic route to Fremont. "The rolling green hills, with vineyards and wineries, are worth a few extra miles," she said. When they reached Fremont, she directed him to turn onto Highway 17, saying, "This will lead us through San Jose and into Los Gatos. If you were to continue west on 17, you would cross the Santa Cruz Mountains and run right into the Pacific Ocean."

Peter laughed. "I don't think we want to go for a swim in the ocean today."   When they reached Los Gatos, Ruth directed him to Main Street and past Los Gatos High School so that he could see where she had been educated. They parked nearby and walked past quaint shops to The Boulangerie on the corner, where they stopped for rolls and coffee.

"See the park across the street? I saw Evan there last summer at a concert and later at the Wine Cellar just around the corner. We were high school and college acquaintances and became reacquainted when fate brought us together."

"Did you fall head over heels in love with him, Ruth?"

"Not quite. I found him extremely attractive, with Hollywood looks, but I didn't exactly fall for him. He had to reel me in, like a fish on a line: first, a picnic on an ocean bluff near Carmel; then a trip to Oakland, where he introduced me to his mission; next, a trip to the center to meet Reverend Howard and **you**; then a trip to Sacramento to see his animal shelter; and finally, a trip to Lake Tahoe, where he attempted to interest me in a plot of land. That was the point at which I suspected his motives."

Peter responded that Evan was adept at convincing others that he was good and wanted to help the poor and the abandoned. "Wily, like the devil," Peter added.

"You saw through him, didn't you?" asked Ruth.

"Not right away. He was skilled at the art of deception."

"At what point did you begin to suspect his true nature?"

"That Sunday when you, Dr. Sandler, Gloria, and I were having lunch in the garden. Evan interrupted us to give you a photo of himself and you standing before the Delta King."

"Yes. He took that picture on our date to Old Sacramento."

"Well, I thought that he treated both you and Gloria badly at the lunch table. Also, he ignored Dr. Sandler and me, treating us as though we didn't exist."

"I didn't notice that," said Ruth.

"You were too busy noticing Evan."

"When did you and Reverend Howard begin to suspect that he was a scam artist?" Ruth asked.

"When he began spending a lot of time soliciting funds for his charities. Reverend asked Edith to keep an eye out for unusual activity in the accounts of the residents."

"When did Reverend Howard hire Earl to investigate Evan?"

"After Edith reported heavy withdrawals from Gloria's account. When Earl came on board, things began to move quickly. Earl gathered evidence of Evan's dishonest schemes."

"At what point did Evan become suspicious that he was being investigated?"

"I'm not sure. He was good at keeping a low profile, but he realized soon enough to avoid arrest."

"Where do you think he has gone?"

"There is no record of his passport having been used, so he must still be in the country."

"Or not. He could have simply walked across the southern border." Peter agreed. Ruth admitted that she had mixed feelings about Evan. "I regret that I dated him, but if I hadn't, I never would have met **you**, Peter."

Peter smiled. "Sometimes evil leads to more evil, but sometimes good follows. Ruth, let's try to put thoughts of Evan out of our minds. Don't let him ruin our weekend."

They left The Boulangerie and drove to the Martin home on Kennedy Road. Ruth's parents were waiting for them. Ruth introduced Peter to her father, whom he had not yet met. She reached out to her mother with an embrace. As Posie yapped a welcome, Ruth picked her up and said, "Meet our precious Posie." Mrs. Martin said, "Ruth, take Peter around to acquaint him with the house, and then help him to get set up in the guest bedroom. When you come back down, join us for snacks and drinks in the lounge."

When they returned, Mrs. Martin wheeled in a trolley holding tiny quiches and a platter of meats, cheeses, pickled vegetables, and slices of apple. Mr. Martin popped the cork from a bottle of champagne and handed out glasses of it, saying, "To Peter and Ruth, may you enjoy your weekend with us." Eager to get to know Peter, Ruth's parents encouraged him to talk about himself.

Peter described growing up in Tucson and remaining with his parents until he graduated from the University of Arizona, then studying at St. Paul Seminary for several years.

"To become a minister?" asked Mr. Martin.

"Yes, at first. Later, I decided that I was better suited for counseling than preaching. When I completed my master's degree, I took the position at the center; two years later, Ruth joined the staff." He reached out for her hand.

"Tell us about your family, Peter," encouraged Mrs. Martin.

"My parents were both teachers in the Tucson Public Schools."

"Were?"

"Yes. They're retired now."

"Ruth told us about your father's accident and his coma. That was an emotional time for your family."

"Yes. I had to leave suddenly to be with my mother and my two brothers at his bedside. Two days later, he came out of the coma and is now beginning to recuperate."

"So, you are one of three children."

"Yes, my older brother is a history professor at U of A in Tucson, and my younger brother is a lieutenant in the army, stationed at San Antonio. When I was home, I told them about Ruth, and they are anxious to meet her." He squeezed Ruth's hand again.

Ruth entered the conversation. "Peter, I told Mom and Dad all about Evan's dishonesty and your part in undertaking a mission to help Reverend Howard."

"Well done, Peter," said Mrs. Martin. "I suspected Evan from the beginning. He seemed too sure of himself."

"We were wondering why Reverend Howard sent you on a mission to Canada, Peter," said Mr. Martin.

"The police and prosecutor were getting close to an arrest, and Evan was getting suspicious. I agreed to be a decoy so that Evan would think that I was under investigation. Reverend Howard let me choose where to spend my leave of absence, and I had always wanted to spend time in the Canadian Rockies. It was a good choice. It was beautiful and peaceful, and it gave me an opportunity to think about my future and about Ruth." He squeezed Ruth's hand again.

"You must be getting tired of all of these questions, Peter. Ruth, why don't you play piano for us?" Ruth willingly played a piece by Satie, with a slow, lyrical melody and an accompaniment of broken chords; she followed it with a lively Chopin polonaise. "Do you like songs from stage shows?" Mrs. Martin asked. Peter's affirmation led to a medley of songs from *South Pacific, Carousel, My Fair Lady*, and *The Sound of Music*, while Ruth's father and mother hummed along.

Mrs. Martin continued to manage the visit. "I have cooking to attend to in the kitchen, and Dad needs to set up the table on the patio and get the fire started on the grill for steaks. Enjoy your time alone," she said to Ruth and Peter.

Ruth suggested playing cards and asked if Peter was familiar with 'Knock-out Whist.'

"No," he answered. "Does one of us get knocked out?"

"You will. I'm very adept at playing cards."

Following dinner, the two couples played a game of hearts, *boys against girls* (the girls won); then a game of Monopoly, *each player for himself* (Mr. Martin bankrupted his opponents). When evening approached and lights came on in the outside yard, Mrs. Martin said, "Dad and I are going up to bed. Why don't you two go out into the garden and enjoy the evening air? Take Posie with you for a stroll." Posie, hearing her name, wagged her tail in anticipation.

Chapter XXIV: The Garden

Ruth followed her mother's suggestion and led Peter outside. It was dusk; the air was warm, and the garden glowed in the light of the setting sun. Peter scanned the expanse of the yard, with its native redwood and oak trees. Here and there, flowering fruit trees had been planted for splashes of pink, rose, and purple.

"Is this an acre of land?" Peter asked.

"Slightly more. My parents wanted to build on a plot of land that was big enough for a house, patio, swimming pool, outdoor kitchen, large lawn, playground, and garden. Let me show you around."

Ruth started the tour near the porch, where the outdoor kitchen was located, which included a brick grill and oven, a refrigerator, a sink and counter space, and enough cupboards and shelves to store food supplies, utensils, and dishes. "My parents enjoy hosting parties here in the garden," she commented. Next, she led him to the pool and patio, a cheerful area with bright umbrellas, tables, and chairs. Large Mexican pots around the pool were planted with snapdragons, Gerbera daisies, pansies, and alyssum. She motioned to a corner of the garden, saying, "That area was formerly a play area, with a slide, swings, and a sandbox. When I grew up, Dad had the play equipment removed and replaced it with a trellis. Around it, lavender rhododendron, white camellias, and pink and rose azaleas were planted."

"Glorious!" remarked Peter.

"In the opposite corner," continued Ruth, "is my favorite tree, the magnolia. I love its shiny leaves and huge white blossoms. The birdbath in front of it, flanked by the large statues of cats, is a safe spot for birds to drink and flutter about in the water. They have no fear of the stone cats."

"How does Posie react to the birds?"

"She ignores them. She's more interested in nosing through the herb bed. Mom had that planted for fresh leaves of oregano, thyme, and marjoram to use in food preparation. When Posie has been rolling around in the herb bed, she smells like pizza."

Peter laughed. "I see that you have a rose garden. Who takes care of the roses?"

"My mother; she won't let the gardener touch it."

"Your mother and father are lovely people, Ruth. No wonder you grew into the woman I love." Taking her in his arms, he said, "Ruth Martin, you must realize by now that I'd love you to become Ruth Paulson."

"Peter Paulson! When did you decide that?"

"I've been thinking about it for some time."

"Oh? When did you first begin to love me?"

"When we were in the chapel, after our group discussion about creation. I suddenly realized that we are *kindred spirits*. He paused. "Ruth, when did **you** begin to love **me**?"

"Not long after that. I was at home visiting my parents. I told them that you had called me a *kindred spirit*, and Dad went to our big Webster dictionary and read the definition of *kindred* in its verb, noun, and adjective forms. That started me thinking that you and I might be headed for love."

"You and your parents are unique, Ruth. May I join your family?"

"I can tell that my mom and dad have already accepted you; so, Ruth Paulson it will be." Peter pulled her closely, and they kissed passionately. "Mrs. Peter Paulson," he repeated softly. When Ruth could catch her breath, she said, "We should tell my parents tomorrow; but perhaps, we should figure out a few elementary plans tonight." Peter agreed. Ruth pointed to a swinging loveseat near the pool and suggested that they sit there to make their plans. Posie followed them and made a threesome as they snuggled together on the loveseat.

By this time, dusk had turned into night. The lights from the pool and the perfume of the night-blooming jasmine were exotic for the two lovers. Together, they decided that a late summer or early fall wedding would be best, giving them time to find a new location to live and work. "The center is not a good place for a young married couple," said Peter. "We will want privacy to adjust to married life."

"Yes," agreed Ruth. "We will need time, too, to send out our resumes, interview prospective employers, and rent a house or apartment. The wedding, itself, will require considerable planning."

"What do you think, Ruth, about a garden setting for our wedding?"

"There's nothing more I would love than getting married right here. There's room in the garden for about 150 guests. The trellis in the corner would make a good spot for the ceremony. We could set up folding chairs on either side of a path leading from the house to the trellis."

"I can picture you, in a white gown, walking down the path with your father."

"I'm sure that Mom and Dad will like the idea. In fact, Mom will want to help us to work out the details. Do you think that your family would mind traveling here for the wedding?"

"Absolutely not. My parents will be anxious to meet yours."

The following morning, Mrs. Martin had breakfast ready in the garden. They served themselves from covered containers of scrambled eggs, cottage potatoes, bacon, and warm toast. Coffee, juice, and cantaloupe were on the table. When they had finished eating, Peter announced: "I proposed to your daughter last night," and Ruth added, "and I accepted."

"Thank God!" said her mother. "Yes, thank God!" repeated her father. Pointing to his wife, he said, "Cupid, here, was hoping for that when she suggested a walk in the garden."

"Guilty," admitted Cupid.

Ruth informed them of the preliminary plans that Peter and she had made concerning their wedding. "Do you have any objection to our having the ceremony and the reception here in the garden?" she asked.

"Certainly not," responded her mother. "You two love birds deserve a garden setting before you fly off to establish your own nest."

"Welcome to the family, Peter!" Mr. Martin extended his hand and followed it with a hug.

Chapter XXV: Dreaming

As Ruth and Peter left Los Gatos, Peter remarked that the garden at the Martins was the most beautiful home garden that he had ever seen. "Aside from its beauty, Ruth, why do you love it so much?"

"Now that I'm no longer a child, I find the garden a place of serenity. It's like the chapel at the center. It inspires me to think about God's creation and His establishing an orderly cycle of nature to sustain life. The garden symbolizes birth, growth, death, and rebirth. So, it strengthens my belief in resurrection from the dead into eternal life."

"And yet, Ruth, some people see an incomplete cycle of life for themselves, ending with dust returning to dust."

"To me," she continued, "that is a hopeless end to life. I prefer to live in anticipation of someday meeting my Maker."

"It comes down to a belief in Christ and the resurrection, which Christians have," said Peter. "You're a deep spiritual thinker, Ruth. You would make a good minister's wife."

"Well, I plan to marry a Christian counselor, who was once a seminarian."

"Would you still be willing to marry me if I decided to go back to the seminary to become a minister? Reverend Howard has suggested that to me more than once."

"I would marry you whatever you want to do when we leave the center. Do you think that you are being called to take that route?"

"I'm not sure. Perhaps Reverend Howard **is the call**."

"You'll eventually know, Peter."

"Yes. In the meantime, you and I can begin our own congregation, starting with one. We haven't talked yet about raising a family; but after seeing your relationship with your parents, Ruth, I feel that you would be a fine mother."

"I've always wanted a sister or brother. Did you like being the middle child of three?"

"I don't think that the number of children or the position within the family has much to do with it. Loving each child and encouraging them to love each other is what's important." He paused and winked at her. "So, let's have twenty kids, Ruth."

"Like J. S. Bach. He had twelve with his first wife and eight more with his second. However, his first wife died after giving birth to the twelfth."

"O.K., Ruth. We'll stop at eleven."

"**You** have the kids, Peter. It's a transgender society."

"Seriously, would you like a diamond ring to show that we are engaged?"

"Yes. I like tradition."

"O.K. We'll go to a jewelry store in Lodi next weekend to choose a diamond ring and two wedding bands."

"Until then, let's keep our engagement secret."

As they reached the canal road and were heading towards the center, Peter said, "The next few months can't go by quickly enough for me."

After he had pulled into the driveway and parked Ruth's car, he retrieved the luggage from the trunk and escorted Ruth up the path to the front door. When they entered, they noticed Cindy sitting in the lounge. She watched them as they checked their mailboxes.

"Just junk mail," commented Ruth.

"Hey, Ruth and Peter," Cindy called to them from the lounge. "Where have you been? We missed you."

"In a garden," answered Ruth.

Cindy looked puzzled. "What kind of garden?"

"The kind I've been looking for," answered Peter.

THE END

Discussion Questions

The novel intertwines several narratives. It is primarily a "rim" story: the outer story of Ruth, Peter, and Evan, and the inner story of "The Creation and the Fall from Paradise." Within the outer story are the diverging tales of Ruth and Evan versus Ruth and Peter. Both of the outer and inner stories deal with the struggle between good and evil.

1. The author alternates between two settings: Los Gatos, Ca. and the delta region in San Joaquin County. Why does the main character, Ruth, leave Los Gatos for the delta?
2. Ruth and Evan become reacquainted by chance. Which of Evan's characteristics attract Ruth?
3. Which characteristics are Ruth's parents skeptical of?
4. Mrs. Martin sees Ruth as accomplished, capable, tender-hearted, loving, and naïve. Do you agree with her mother's assessment?
5. When Ruth first meets Peter, she sees him as an average man – in appearance and personality. As she learns to know him, she discovers his superior qualities. What are they?
6. Evan sees Peter as a rival. How does Evan show his dislike for Peter?
7. Ruth learns to know Evan through their dates to various places. What does she learn about him from the trip to Oakland and San Francisco? About him from the trip to Sacramento? The trip to Lake Tahoe?

Through the group discussions at the "center," Ruth realizes that Peter is a man devoted to loving God and helping his neighbor. She learns that he is a leader who not only has a good knowledge of theology and the Bible but has the ability to guide others to a better understanding and love of God.

8. How does Peter help Ruth to become a leader?
9. Peter and Ruth share the leadership role according to a basic goal proposed by Peter. The topics of the first two discussions are

'angels' and 'devils.' What did you think after the group discussion?

    a. Did God create angels before man?

    b. Do good angels and bad angels exist today?

    c. According to The Bible, how does God use the good angels?

10. The Creation and the Fall from Paradise are the topics of the 3rd and 4th discussions. What do you think?

    a. Did God create the world, or did it happen by chance?

    b. Was man created in God's image? Explain.

    c. Was Paradise destroyed by man's disobedience to God?

    d. According to 'Genesis,' God has denied man eternal life, except by divine intervention. Explain.

11. Which of the residents in the group have the best understanding of the topics that are discussed? Which have the least?

12. What parallels do you see between the serpent in Paradise and Evan?

13. When Evan flees, he leaves behind victims who have lost money, reputation, and honor. Who is hurt the most by his duplicity and selfishness?

14. Is Gloria in any way responsible for Evan's character? Explain.

15. Ruth moved from the security of a loving family to begin a life on her own, to seek success in her career and happiness in her personal life. Did she find them?

16. At the end of the story, Ruth has lost her naivete and has gained a better understanding of good and evil. Has Peter's love enriched her life and strengthened her faith in God?

17. Is it likely that Peter will become a minister?

18. Throughout the story, Ruth and Peter have sought the garden as a place to meditate, to commune with God and each other, and to enjoy its beauty. In what ways might the garden symbolize their new life together?

References:

The King James Study Bible

Reverend Timothy Keller, *The Reason for God*

Kent A. Kiehl, Ph.D., *Psychopath Whisperer*

Frank G. Anderson, M.D., *Transcending Trauma*

Richard Gallagher, M.D., *Demonic Foes*

C. S. Lewis, author and Oxford professor,

> *A Preface to Paradise Lost,*
> *The Problem of Pain,*
> *The Screwtape Letters*

John Milton, 17th century author, *Paradise Lost*

Article in AARP Magazine, January 2024,

> "The Extraordinary World of Music and the Mind," by John Colapinto

DVDs: *The Bishop's Wife, Kismet, Brigadoon*

About the Author:

Fauneil was born and raised in rural Nebraska. From childhood, she has been interested in education, both seeking learning for herself and imparting it to others. She has four degrees: B.Sc. in Ed., University of Nebraska; M.Ed., University of Arizona; B.A. and M.A., San Jose State University. She has traveled throughout the U. S., Canada, and Europe and has lived and worked in five states: Nebraska, Arizona, New Mexico, Texas, and California.

In her lifetime, she has had three careers: (1) as a teacher of English and music, (2) as a church organist, and (3) as a writer. Since 2019, she has published the following books:

I Didn't Really Know Him, 2019 – Beth, a widow, adjusts to the death of her husband. In the process, she learns that "God is love."

The Seeds of the Prairie, 2021 – The lives of three Christian immigrant families become intertwined through faith, hard work, companionship, and love.

Walter and Lisetta: Living, Loving, Learning, 2022 – *Walter and Lisetta raise their family during The Great Depression and World War II. Lisetta, the peacemaker, holds the family together amid their problems, setting an example of caring and love.*

Confused and Abused, 2023 - *Brio is the victim of the scammer, Richie, at a time of loneliness after her move to Texas. She gradually learns that he is adept at manipulating her and that she must escape from his control before it is too late.*

www.ingramcontent.com/pod-product-compliance
Lightning Source LLC
Chambersburg PA
CBHW081004140626
46546CB00019B/3303